shifting
shorelines

shifting shorelines

Messages from a Wiser Self

An ode to nature, the passage of time,
and the ripening of wisdom

terry helwig

Published in the United States by Viva Editions, an imprint of Start Midnight, LLC, 221 River Street, Ninth Floor, Hoboken, New Jersey 07030.

Printed in the United States
Cover design: Jennifer Do
Cover image: Shutterstock
Text design: Frank Wiedemann

First Edition.
10 9 8 7 6 5 4 3 2 1

Trade paper ISBN: 978-1-63228-072-5
E-book ISBN: 978-1-63228-129-6

Excerpt from *Praise Song for the Pandemic*, © Christine Valters Paintner, used with permission from the author, Abbeyofthearts.com.

For my sister, Nancy; I will meet you in the field, beyond right and wrong.[1]

I was thus filled with longing to behold . . . the splendours . . .
To witness the Ocean gathered up into a drop.

—RUMI[2]

TABLE OF CONTENTS

INTRODUCTION

*I*n my imagination, surf swirls about my ankles. In the distance, I see a woman standing, looking out to sea. Something about her feels familiar. She turns, meets my eyes, and smiles. Then it dawns on me. She is me at a younger age. I recognize her, but she has no recognition of me. I drink in the sight of her and her youth, knowing only too well the expression she wears on her face.

She turns back toward the sea, standing as still as an egret, seeking some sort of synchronicity or sign to guide her: a dolphin surfacing, an osprey flying overhead, even a rainbow on the horizon. I know the earnestness of her heart and the weight of her unnecessary angst as she beseeches the Universe for guidance.

I long to speak with her—tell her what I know and what I have learned. I have weathered the tides she is about to encounter and walked the shoreline ahead of her. I have seen the world, not only through her eyes, but also through the lens of time.

Today, in the salty air of morning, seagulls gossip and circle a dozen brown pelicans. Schools of frenzied fish roil the waters. One opportunistic gull perches, clown-like, atop the head of a floating pelican, hoping a fish will escape the pelican's accordion-like pouch. No luck. The pelican swallows and finishes with an end-of-meal tail wag that I have witnessed a thousand times on a thousand walks.

For the better part of forty years, I have left footprints upon the warm, white sand currently shifting beneath my feet. This four-mile stretch of beach curls, ribbon-like, around a blue jewel—the Gulf of Mexico. The Tewa people of New Mexico believe they are massaging the earth when they walk upon her. It's lovely to think my morning walks along this damp shore massage the earth, because I love this barrier island. This book is, in part, an ode to life beside the sea.

But, more importantly, this book is an effort to care for the soul; it is an ode to the rising and falling tides of life and time, an exploration of the ripening of wisdom.

As I walk north into my seventies, I remember the angst of my thirties, forties, and fifties. I was that younger woman, looking out to sea, earnestly beseeching the Universe for answers and direction. While my concerns—career, healing childhood trauma, more education, becoming a parent, relocating—weren't life threatening, they were life altering. They loomed large and solid in my psyche. It is only now, in hindsight, that I see those issues eventually dissolved into time, much like sandcastles ebbing with the tide. It was my tightly wound angst that never dissolved; it merely changed shape to cloak yet another concern.

Would that I could slip my arm around my younger self, teasing that the dress code for life does not require such angst. I would pull her close and whisper, *"Listen . . . I have something to tell you."*

A deep well of lived experience resides within each of us. Throughout these pages, at the end of each chapter, a short, italicized message gives voice to this lived experience. These messages are meant to comfort, encourage, and inspire—not only my younger self, but also my daughter, and all the sons and daughters before and after her. I invite you, as you read, to write messages of your own, drawing from your own experience. How has wisdom ripened within you? What messages of comfort and hope might you share from the shifting shoreline of your own life?*

This book is divided into three sections that reflect the timeless flow of tides:

I. Ebb Tide, the first section, reflects times of loss and sadness; it pertains to the outflow of life. During ebb tides, the ocean recedes farthest from the shore, laying bare a wide stretch of beach that may strand some sea life. In the psyche, ebb tides lay bare a wide swath of grief that sometimes strands hope and healing.

II. Slack Tide, the second section, points to a time of standstill—a time of contentment, contemplation, and being. During slack tides, the water is almost motionless, perfectly balanced between the inflow and outflow of seawater. In the psyche, slack tides are the soft sighs of respite, a time to take stock and reflect.

---

* The last chapter, "Ponder This," includes questions and a study guide for individuals and groups.

III. Flood Tide, the final section of the book, focuses on times of fullness and gratitude. During flood tides, the water rises toward the dunes, erasing footprints and sandcastles. Flood tides swell toward the shore, smoothing gouged-out places and wiping the slate clean to begin anew. In the psyche, flood tides are small epiphanies, treasured moments of well-being that swell the heart with love and gratitude.

The dance of these perpetual tides changes the contour of our lives, continually shifting the shoreline of who we are and, more importantly, who we will become.

Peace of the falling wave to you,
Terry Helwig

EBB TIDE

*The period during
which water flows
away from the shore*

*When anxious, uneasy and bad thoughts come, I go to the sea,
and the sea drowns them out with its great wide sounds, cleanses
me with its noise and imposes a rhythm upon everything in me
that is bewildered and confused.*

—RAINER MARIA RILKE[3]

MI ISLA

I smell of sunscreen, and perspiration beads on my brow, the result of corkscrewing a hibiscus-pink umbrella stand twelve inches into the sand. Here, at the water's edge, a sea breeze flutters my bangs. I secure the umbrella, win the tussle with my salt-corroded beach chair that creaks into submission, and ferret out my writing journal and Spanish class workbook. Admittedly, I don't open either one for the better part of an hour. I simply sit and stare at the waves, allowing my mind to wander and drift like the coconut wobbling in the tide before me, destined for a distant shore.

The only Spanish I can conjure up this sultry afternoon is: *Quiero nadar.* I want to swim.

The outgoing tide has created a wide swath of beach. I wade into the Gulf, warm water lapping against my knees as I shuffle my feet to shoo away any stingrays that may have buried themselves beneath the sand. Stingrays are, by nature, docile creatures, attacking with their barbed tail only when they feel threatened, like being stepped on. I have seen their dark, V-shaped shadows glide silently beneath the undulating waves many times; I have never once, in forty years, been bothered.

The sandy bottom dips away and I bob in the current, like a lazy buoy at sea. Frigatebirds glide overhead, suspended on air currents, without so much as a single flap of their wings, just the tilt of a wing feather here and there. I am forever in awe of the long-tailed frigates, a little jealous, even. Solar-powered transmitters have tracked some of these birds aloft for two months at a time, never once alighting, eating and sleeping on the wing; they fly on average 255 miles daily.[4] What freedom, soaring unencumbered above the sea in thermals and tropical breezes.

I cannot ride the thermals, but I can and do enjoy the tropical breezes—one of many things bonding me to this island. Salt water splashes my lips. The divide between my growing-up years in West Texas and this island overwhelms me at times. My five younger sisters and I lived with our parents in a ten-foot-by-sixty-foot trailer. The good thing about living in a trailer is that it can be easily moved. The bad thing about living in a trailer is that it can be easily moved.

Always the proverbial new girl, I attended twelve schools, in twelve different towns, before my high school graduation. Daddy's oil-exploration job required him and his diamond bits to drill core samples in hundreds of remote fields in the big-sky country of the American Southwest. Daddy searched for crude oil, created by plankton in ancient seas, and I searched for something just as remote—a cure for Mama.

Mom married numerous times, twice to Daddy, and she often found solace in bars at night. It was a neighbor child who informed me, with some certitude, that Mama was a "playgirl." When I questioned Mama about this, she tightened her jaw and steeled her hazel eyes. "Nosy neighbors!" she said. "Don't pay them any mind."

Mostly, I didn't pay the neighbors any mind. As the oldest child, I had plenty of chores and homework to keep me distracted. But at night, after my sisters and I had made dinner, done the dishes, and put the little ones to bed, I would lie in bed wishing for a different kind of life; one with a mom who didn't hang out at bars and swallow so many pills. I wanted a mom more like June Cleaver, a mom who tucked me in at night and made fresh-baked cookies.

Then, somewhere along the line, I traded in June Cleaver for the life of a castaway, probably after reading Daniel Defoe's *Robinson Crusoe* and Johann David Wyss's *The Swiss Family Robinson*. The thought of living on a deserted island became a balm for my troubles.

Night after night, I visited my imaginary island. I feared nothing there on the sunlit shore. Strong, happy, and tanned, I built a tree house in my imagination from debris that washed ashore, including a canvas sail that I hung as a hammock for my bed. I fashioned make-believe ropes and shells into room dividers and planks of waterlogged lumber into a bench and picnic table, just like the one Daddy built for our trailer. Fragrant flowers rested in coconut bowls. From my tree house bed, I could watch falling stars and gaze upon the moon. I ordered my world, on my beautiful island, in ways that I could never order my world in real life.

The hours I spent conjuring up my island sanctuary were legion. I visited there for many years. But it wasn't until I was a young mom, visiting Disney World's Swiss Family

Robinson tree house for the first time, that a familiar feeling washed over me. Seeing the tidied, makeshift rooms of the tree house, running my hands across the rough ropes and limbs, admiring the picnic-like table, covered with books— all the memories of my imaginary island swept over me.

My knees actually buckled.

"You okay?" my husband, Jim, asked.

I nodded, wondering how to convey the tidal wave of insight that suddenly overwhelmed me. I had never connected the dots. How did I not see it? My childhood fantasy, the one I thought I had outgrown, the one I had thrown onto the trash heap of adulthood, had come true. Those many hours spent conjuring up an island had come to fruition.

I now live on an island, and, evidently, not entirely by happenstance. Like the frigates, riding the currents, adjusting a wing feather here and there, my longing and countless hours of visualization must have created thermals and currents that helped lead me here. My island is not deserted, but the ten thousand islands surrounding it *are*. I visit some of these deserted shores by boat and kayak, leaving only footprints in the sand. I do not sleep in a canvas-sail bed, but I do watch falling stars and gaze upon the moon.

Don't ever doubt the power of your thoughts, I would tell my younger self. Don't squander them on anger, hopelessness, worry, or regret. Instead, bind your thoughts together with ropes of hope and determination. Use them to build a dream; dreams can keep you aloft for months, even years. They can help you soar above your circumstances and sustain yourself on the wing.

If repeated thoughts and dreams can manifest in our three-dimensional world, make sure to tend your dreams with care. Continually visualize yourself where you want to be; let yourself feel the textures of the life you seek. Feel the roughness of a canvas-sail bed; allow your eyes to look outward from the place of your dreams. If you long for something, picture yourself already there. You have control of what you yearn for; don't invite doubt to join you. Send him on his way. He knows not of thermals and currents that can lift a wing and help it soar.

Salt water splashes my legs as I shuffle back to the shore. Rivulets of water stream down my body and disappear into my thirsty beach towel. My salt-corroded beach chair creaks under my weight. Tucked into my circle of shade, on my longed-for island, with the wide expanse of beach before me, I open my writing journal and pick up my pen.

Mi Isla . . . I begin.

SEA JEWEL

The sun yawns in the east, sending soft morning rays to illumine the various treasures dropped by the waves overnight. Different treasures get washed ashore with different tides, which is true this morning. I glimpse something unusual peeking through the bulbous seaweed. Using my staff of driftwood, I poke and crunch through the mound of seaweed, pen shells, and decaying sea urchins—the urchins' spiny carcasses off-gassing an ammonia smell with such pungency that my eyes water.

Despite the nose-wrinkling odor, I bend and pick up a marble-size, silver-gray orb of loveliness that feels both hard and silky-smooth, almost jewel-like, between my fingertips. I have been shelling for years, but I've never seen anything like this. It is hollow and weighs less than a dime, but it is neither a shell nor a stone. Still, I have no doubt that it belongs to the sea.

What can it be?

Another morning shell collector, already laden with a bulging bag of specimens, looks my way and playfully holds her nose. I smile and nod in agreement, then, holding up my find, I ask, "Do you happen to know what this is?"

She approaches, takes the orb into her palm, and rolls it around like a roly-poly, poking it with her finger. "I don't have a clue," she says, handing it back to me. "Sorry." Her eyes meet mine. "You found it here?"

I nod. "A mystery to be unraveled," I say, then I turn toward an outcropping of rocks.

"Good luck," she calls after me.

I palm my newfound gift and perch on my favorite boulder. I come here to contemplate both life and the sea. Sitting on a boulder that has made the acquaintance of a million waves is a privilege not lost on me. I am a naturalist at heart, in love with stones, animals, trees, shells, mountains, deserts, and the sea. I find tremendous beauty, solace, and meaning in the outer world in which I live.

And yet, I pursued a master's degree in psychology. While I am insatiably curious about all flora and fauna, especially on this barrier island, I am just as curious about the unseen, inner world of the psyche and soul. I believe our inner and outer worlds mirror one another and, when braided together, they create both well-being and mystery. Like the symbiotic relationship between roots and leaves, the inner and outer landscapes of life can coalesce into a mysterious blend of meaning and synchronicity, leading to new ways of being. Instead of observing a static world, we can become participants in a dynamic unfolding universe. This is where I choose to live.

I didn't always live this way. There was a time when I fought very hard to keep a lid on my feelings. I prided myself on being a strong person and not showing any signs of weakness or vulnerability. It wasn't until I became interested in Jungian psychology that I decided to lift that lid and venture in. I remember telling myself not to worry: "You'll be okay even if you aren't okay."

Oddly, this assurance gave me a great sense of peace. I took a deep breath, waded in, and didn't look back. My feelings and actions became more congruent; I felt more authentically me. All the energy I expended *keeping a lid on things* was freed up. I discovered new interests, felt more creative, and experienced a deep sense of calm and well-being. The same calm and well-being I feel now.

My thoughts entrain with the hypnotic rising and falling of the waves until my left leg begins to tingle from the pressure of sitting too long on the boulder. A wave crashes against the rocks and sends sea mist swirling in the air about me, tickling my cheeks with spray. Brushing gritty sand from my backside, I carry my mysterious jewel back to the condo.

Curious, I heft down several shell books from the living-room shelf. Sprawling them across the kitchen table, I thumb through numerous pages, finally coming upon a section called *Other Beach Life*. There between a picture of a whelk-shell egg case and spiny sea urchin, I spot my prize.

It seems I am in possession of a sea pearl, not of the oyster variety.

Combing the internet, I discover that my pearl is actually a sea bean, a variety of drift seed, belonging to the tropical, hard-to-pronounce leguminous tree *Caesalpinia bonduc*, more commonly known as the warri tree. The soft, green warri seeds eventually fall from the parent tree and calcify into stone-smooth gray seeds. High tides carry the fallen seeds into the sea, where they may bob and drift on ocean currents for months, even years, before washing ashore in faraway places like the Orkney Islands, or Scandinavia, or, evidently, my small island beside the sea.

I turn the pearl over and over in my fingertips, imagining it bobbing for miles, possibly years. When did it harden like porcelain and turn gray? How long and how far has it traveled? No wonder people, for centuries, valued finding one. Not only was a sea pearl considered a prized amulet of good luck, childbirth, healing, and longevity, some cultures even ground the seeds to treat malaria, earning it the moniker *quinine of the poor.*[5]

I most resonate with the idea of it being a talisman of longevity. In my outer world, I have discovered a sea pearl, but, in my inner world, I have stumbled upon a perfect amulet of longevity. What better talisman for aging than an exotic, lovely, turning-gray jewel? I find the story of its ripening beautiful and compelling.

When I attempt to display the pearl in my wooden bowl of prized shells, it gets lost, overshadowed by the glossy conch, tulip, and cone shells. It's too small to stand alone among my large whelks, angel wings, and sea urchins lining the kitchen shelf. Then I think of the three-dimensional plaque hanging above my desk in my office. Some years ago, I came across a Greek plaster relief of a blue-gowned Hebe, the cupbearer, who was said to feed ambrosia and nectar to the gods. In one hand, Hebe carries a vase and, in the other, she holds out a small shallow bowl in which to pour her nectar, hollowed just enough that it might actually hold my jewel.

The pearl fits perfectly, as if Hebe's sculptor had created the relief for this very purpose. I smile, quite pleased with myself to find such an apropos location. After one last admiring look, I turn and catch myself still smiling in the carved white mirror hanging on the adjacent wall. These days, I almost don't recognize the matured reflection smiling back at me.

Stepping closer, I gaze into my dark-brown eyes. Somewhere, deep inside me, there resides a remnant of the soft and green young woman I used to be, a young, earnestly seeking woman trying to keep a lid on things, a young woman as smooth-skinned as Hebe, offering up her nectar to life. I never imagined, back then, that the swift current of life would beach me, so soon, on this lovely island where I now reside, quite content, but far, far away from youth. I think of her, now, that young woman in my imagination, standing as still as an egret beside the sea.

What you don't understand, I would tell that younger version of myself, is that you will always feel very green inside, even when the mirror ceases to reflect that greenness. What matters is the ripening of wisdom, the ripening of the soul, not the physical changes of flesh. Treasure your need-to-lose-five-pounds body now, because someday you will weep because you did not love it enough. Those faint lines creasing your face—they are human tree rings, calculating your years on earth; they have nothing to do with the sap within you.

Aging is a costume you will be made to wear. It is the price of ripening wisdom, but, inside the gray hair, creased lines, and puffy eyes, you will feel the "you" you have always been. Aging is a hard-to-understand cosmic joke that finally dawns on you when you look into a mirror and wonder: Who are you? The dichotomy between the body you see and the Self you feel reveals itself in that moment.

Your body wears the costume of elderhood, and, when your last breath is drawn, that costume will be laid aside. But your eternal Self, pooled behind the iris of your eyes, can never be touched by time.

And when you are in the presence of elders, remember: don't be fooled by age's costume. Look deep into their eyes, where the eternal Self dwells; they are ripened souls, spiritual beings who have walked this earth longer than most.

Months later, after placing my sea pearl in Hebe's outstretched palm, I experienced an aha moment. I learned, quite by accident, that Hebe's name comes from the Greek word for youth. Not only was Hebe a mythological cupbearer to the gods, she also had the ability to restore youth. It is she who holds my sea pearl.

How perfect is that?

Leaving home, falling from the parent tree, bobbing in life's currents, and eventually washing ashore: therein lies the alchemy and nectar of a human life. My sea pearl symbolizes a kind of grace around aging; it highlights the beauty of maturation and the immortality of the soul. Where is the sting of becoming an exotic, ripened, silver-gray orb of loveliness, borne in the palm of youth, and offered up to the world as nectar?

OTTER MOUND

Daddy would likely say that I betrayed him. I see it quite differently.

Even though Daddy is very much alive, in a town thousands of miles away, I have come to say goodbye and bury his ashes. Not his actual ashes, but only the ashes of a burned photograph. Perhaps this burial ritual will rescue me from the cavern of his rejection. I need a quiet space, a sacred place, even, to mourn his absence.

This small hardwood hammock seems a perfect place.

A few moments earlier, I had been sitting, engine idling, in the parking lot of our small island cemetery, surveying the waving flags and flowers dotting the headstones. The cemetery had seemed a logical place for my ritual burial. However, the treeless, grassy knoll felt too open and exposed, the sunlight too glaring. So I drove here, instead, to Otter Mound preserve.

Thankfully, no one is in sight. A paper-thin snake skin dangles from a slash pine near the entrance, a reminder that snakes can be found in the dense vegetation. This is not the first time I have walked this path that winds deeper into the woods. I come, sometimes, to slip beneath the canopy of trees, to disappear for a while and listen to the leaves of the mastics, royal poincianas, and yellow elders whisper to one another.

In addition to the charred paper ashes, I carry a paperback of my memoir *Moonlight on Linoleum*—its publication an apparent embarrassment to Daddy. I walk slowly beneath the trees, wondering if Daddy ever thinks of me. Soft earth and grasses muffle my footsteps.

Beneath the earth and grass lies an ancient shell mound, built and revered by the Calusa Indians. Over time, hundreds of thousands of mussels, oysters, clams, conchs, and whelks, emptied from Calusa baskets, formed the topography of this two-and-one-half-acre mound, rising several stories above sea level. Countless unearthed spiraled whelks, pitted and bone-gray, dot the landscape, reminding me of a sacred boneyard.

Yes, I think to myself, *this space, created in times past, is the perfect place to let go of the past.*

My eyes trace the woody tentacles of a strangler fig, winding and wrapping itself, python-like, around the bark of another tree. In time, the strangler fig will choke the life out of its host tree. I can relate. Even though I try not to let my sadness over losing Daddy eclipse my joy, it sneaks up on me sometimes. Like the day I stumbled upon his picture, embedded in someone's Facebook feed.

Daddy is not on Facebook, but there he was, laughing, beneath an oversize sombrero, celebrating and sharing his birthday at a Mexican restaurant, with his other family. I distinctly remember thinking of him on that very birthday and how odd it felt not to have sent him a card, something I had done every year of my adult life until . . . until what?

Until I received his angry letter.

When I was growing up, Daddy, like Hercules, shouldered my world, and that of my five younger sisters. He was, without question, the pillar upon which our entire family balanced. He was not my birth father, but neither was he just a stepfather; he was my everything father. He fanned my love for the out of doors the same way he stirred campfires, sending embers upward toward the Big Dipper and Milky Way. He flipped pancakes and smelled the kitchen up with bacon on Saturday mornings, he answered my screams and stomped a scorpion in my bedroom, and he always came back for me and my sisters, time and time again, despite Mama's hurtful and often erratic behavior. My sisters and I adored him, which makes my estrangement from him all the more painful.

When I wrote my memoir, I worried about dredging up all the chaos and family dysfunction, but it seemed to me that my book was, essentially, a love letter to Daddy. I was shocked when he disowned me, stunned that he apparently feared people would judge him unfavorably or make fun of him. No one with a heart could possibly laugh at the loving father he had been. Reader after reader told me he was an amazing man.

Evidently Daddy doesn't see it that way. He seems ashamed of the young man he once was. It's as if the years that spanned my entire childhood with him exist in a past he would rather forget.

In my naïveté, I even believed he might be proud. Instead, he wrote a disapproving letter and signed it—not with his familiar signature of *Daddy*, a name I had called him for more than half a century. No, he clenched a pen and signed the letter with his full first and last name, a name I changed in the book, per his request, so no one would recognize the hero of our childhood.

Perhaps my recent years of tiptoeing on the sidelines of his life have made it easier, somehow, for him to let go of the frayed rope that had kept me tenuously moored to his current life and family. I don't know. I only know that reading his letter felt like I had been punched in the stomach and tossed aside, like an empty whelk, clanking onto a shell mound. I started to shake uncontrollably; his words blurred on the paper. The loving pillar, upholding the most stabilized part of my childhood, collapsed into ashes.

I wrote back to him, telling him I adored him and would change his name and all identifying factors, but I never heard from him again. The pain of losing him is deep and raw, strangling even my best memories of him, which is why I can think of only one thing to do: say goodbye.

I stop in front of a large gumbo limbo; its smooth, pink-tinted bark and gracefully arched limbs remind me of a dancing woman. Even though today is not for dancing, I know I have found *the* place. The charred ashes that I pull from my bag come from burning a copy of Daddy's picture. My favorite picture, actually, when Daddy *was* that very young man I wrote about—wearing a white T-shirt and jeans, standing, hands on his hips, in the yard of my grandparents' farm, smiling proudly into the camera.

A mosquito whines near my ear as I step off the path. Bending down, I empty out the charred ashes, mixing them with the dark earth. It feels very much like a funeral. A funeral closes a door; no amount of bloody-knuckle knocking can open that door ever again.

I flip to the back of my memoir and read aloud the last two pages, where I wrote about joy and sorrow being the two sides of love, how life has its tragedies, but also its points of radiance. The Daddy I knew as a child, the one who loved me, the one who first knelt beside me when I was three years old, the one who cried at my high school graduation, will always be a point of radiance in my life. But the other daddy, the one who disowned me, all these years later, is a man I no longer recognize.

Only now do I realize the depth of this schism. Daddy's letter shocked me, actually. With thunderbolt clarity, I finally grasped that the young man I wrote about in my book no longer existed. He had moved on. No amount of longing or wishing could bring him back.

So what does one do in this situation?

I choose to remember the love that was given to me. I am no longer that young girl who needed her daddy to wear a hero's cape. Daddy wore it proudly for many years. I am who I am because of everything that has happened to me. I am a woman watching the sands of the hourglass mound higher; I am a woman ripening with time, and I am a woman who can choose how to respond to hurt and disappointment.

So I choose now to fold up Daddy's cape and say good-bye with love, respect, and gratitude.

Love won't always turn out the way you hope, I would tell my younger self, no matter how tightly you try to grip the fraying rope of a broken relationship. Love is a flowering of the soul. Some loves flower for a lifetime, some for a season, and some more briefly still. Losing love can, indeed, be a razor that cuts deep, but don't allow yourself to bleed to death. Bind your wounds, offer up your pain, and limp forward. It is unremitting grief and bitterness that strangle the life out of us. Grieve, yes, but don't be a host for grief; don't let its tentacles wrap so tightly around you that you cannot survive. Give thanks for the days that love flowered, no matter how briefly. If joy and sorrow are the two sides of love, give them equal space in your heart. Let sorrow hollow out a place for yet more love to flow.

I wipe my dirt-stained hands on my jeans; they smell of ash, reminding me of Daddy's campfires. Sunlight filters through the trees. Standing on the ancient shells, I say goodbye and close the door on the Daddy of my childhood.

INJUSTICE

I bend over a clutch of near-empty beer bottles, carelessly tossed onto the dunes. Stale, warm beer drools onto my hand as I wrinkle my nose and clank the contraband glass bottles into my garbage bag. Whoever brought in the bottles ignored the beach sign that says *No Glass Allowed*. The thought of broken glass gashing bare feet makes my knees weak. I pick up the last bottle, wipe my wet, musty hands onto my capris, and rub the kinks out of my back.

"Thank you," a woman's voice says from behind me. I turn to see a smiling, thirtyish woman, carrying a garbage bag and a long-handled grabber. She, too, is picking up litter. She has, evidently, been watching me.

"I work at the Chamber, and we appreciate people like you," she says.

I swipe at the sweat on my brow with the back of my hand, basking in her praise. "Thanks. My MO occasionally includes a walk on the beach to collect something other than seashells," I tell her.

Collecting beach litter once or twice a month is my way

to repay the sea for what she gives me. In reality, I feel like David, equipped with only a plastic bag, trying to fight Goliath; there are an estimated 5.25 trillion pieces of plastic debris littering the sea.[6] The only solace I take in the face of such a staggering figure is the knowledge that my collected bags of litter do not add to that number.

I tell myself that removing a single plastic bag from the beach might save a sea turtle from mistaking it for a jellyfish. It discourages me to read that over a million marine animals die every year from ingesting plastic[7]—even whales. I was shocked to read about a struggling pilot whale that died; an autopsy revealed it had ingested eighty plastic bags.[8]

Picking up litter in my own backyard is my antidote to apathy. I plan to keep picking it up as long as my back will allow. As it is, I rest my hands on my hips and arch my aching back as I continue talking with the woman from the Chamber.

Unexpectedly, she thrusts her long-handled grabber toward me. "Here," she says, "Keep this; it'll make things easier."

I lift my hands in protest. "Oh, no, I couldn't—"

"The Chamber hands them out sometimes. To people just like you," she insists.

I pause momentarily. My back often aches after my cleanups. Anything to avoid bending over and over would be helpful.

"Thank you," I tell her. "I will make good use of it."

And I have made good use of the grabber. It saves me from stooping over every single piece of trash I collect. It can even pick up something as small as a straw or cigarette butt. Plus, it's more sanitary; no more beer spilling onto my hands.

However, this morning, I am without my trusty grabber and trash bag. I left them in the condo. I had not intended to collect trash on this walk; I only planned to walk for *pure OD* pleasure (an old southern expression that my sister Nancy and I used to mean one hundred percent). But already I am haunted by several salt-corroded aluminum cans, one sun-faded flip-flop, and other debris. It makes no sense to pick up the litter now; I am just starting out on my walk. Hand-carrying so many cumbersome items three miles instead of a mile is illogical. I decide to pick up everything on my way back to the condo, where I will dump it into the trash can near our entry gate.

With my plan in place, I continue walking, empty-handed, until a wave splashes the shore and I see a shiny plastic wrapper, churning in the breakers. I reach down and quickly fish it out, water dribbling down my wrists.

Can't have this going back out to sea, I tell myself. *A turtle might mistake it for a fish.*

Not having a bag, or any pockets, for that matter, I decide to toss the soggy wrapper well above the tide line, far enough away from the surf to make sure it cannot be swept back into the sea before I return to pick it up, along with the other debris.

As soon as I toss the sodden wrapper high up on the sand, I hear a man's gruff voice behind me: "I can't believe people like you."

I spin on the sand, wide-eyed, my hand still dripping with salt water.

Could he possibly be talking to me?

"You make me sick," he says, shaking his head and snatching up the wrapper I just tossed aside.

He has come to the wrong conclusion.

"But I'm—"

"Save the excuses," he says, dismissing me with a wave of his hand, as if swatting away a detestable fly. He strides past me, stuffing the wrapper into his pocket. His graying hair is the only clue to his age.

Unexpectedly, tears well in my eyes. I try again. "I'm not littering, I'm—"

"Leaving it for someone else to pick up," he yells over his shoulder.

His words sting. I stand there, openmouthed, motionless, paralyzed by the tentacles of injustice, unable to run after him, helpless to make him understand.

"I wasn't littering," I say to no one.

There may be times when you are unjustly accused, I would tell my younger self. Injustice stings the soul; it wounds innocence. Imagine, then, what grievous injustices do to the soul—injustices based on skin color, gender, country of origin, religious choice, or economic status. These injustices tear apart the fabric of life. They destroy well-being.

It is not enough to empathize. Injustice wounds so deeply, you must take care not to wield its knife yourself. Judging others, even if it seems you have "caught them in the act," may, in fact, be misjudging them. From the outside looking in, it is hard to know another's heart, or how wrongly you may have misjudged the situation. Err always on the side of compassion.

And should a time arise when you yourself are unjustly accused, stand tall and strong. Don't allow hurtful words and actions to litter

*your life. What others think of you can never change the truth of
who you are, the truth of what you stand for, or the truth of what
you do.*

On my way back, I gather up the beach litter, as I had
planned, and hand-carry it home, sans the plastic wrapper.

NANCY'S PLATE

"My dearest sister," she had written.

Seeing her distinct, left-handed writing makes me miss her all the more. I reread her words, neatly printed, tilting toward the left margin, revealing in their tilt an inkling of her maverick nature:

> *Just a little something from me to you. A small reminder of my eternal love and devotion. And when you choose to use it, for those happy occasions, you will think about how we loved to laugh, and how easy it was to find beauty and humor when in each other's company, and you will smile, remembering. I will love you always.*

> *Your forever sister, Nancy*

The *little something* is a fused, art-glass plate that lives on my hall shelf. I adore it; I pass the plate at least three times a day and, on busy days, as many as two dozen. A close-up sand-dollar motif looks to be embedded within the glass. The design involved a tedious and intricate twenty-hour process of stenciling layers of powdered enamel onto one piece of glass, topping that layer with a second piece of glass, and firing both of them until they melted together.

"Be sure to use it," Nancy had admonished. "Don't keep it just for decoration."

Nancy knew me so well.

She knew I loved serving appetizers and drinks on the terrace—especially at sundown, my favorite time of day, when the ocean and sky embrace in a slow dance to the bending wavelengths of the color spectrum. But Nancy's gift is made of glass; my terrace is tiled in stone. So, despite Nancy's admonition to use the plate, I reasoned it would be safer tucked away securely on my hall shelf.

When I first propped the plate into its stand beside my ceramic inkwells and pen, I realized what I was doing. Not only did I want to protect Nancy's glass plate from breaking, I wanted to protect Nancy. I longed to tuck her away, out of harm's reach, in a place beside my inkwell and pen, where she could not be touched by her stage-4 pancreatic cancer diagnosis. The cancer, already metastasized to her liver, teetered above us like a giant sledgehammer, sure to shatter her future into bits and pieces.

Nancy knew this, too, which is why she wrote, *Think about how we loved to laugh, and how easy it was to find beauty and humor when in each other's company, and you will smile, remembering.*

I do smile. And, sometimes, I cry. On her last visit here, she wore a wide-brimmed hat to cover her balding head. We selected outrageously bright nail polish for our pedicures, we ate decadent entrées at my favorite seaside restaurant, and we snapped a close-up of our gaily painted toes at the water's edge. Her footprints and mine, side by side. I didn't want to think about only one set of footprints.

I was the older sister; all my life I had tried to protect her. Suddenly, I was powerless to help, powerless to safely tuck her out of harm's way and to keep her world from shattering. The only thing I could offer her was my love and my willingness to be present to whatever came next. "There isn't anything I won't talk about," I told her. "I'm strong enough to walk this walk with you."

I had no answers, but I listened, reminded myself to be one hundred percent present, and trusted the present moment enough to say what came to mind.

Nancy's greatest worry was her family: her husband, Barry; her grown children, Kim, Becca, and Kevin; and her grandchildren, Justin and Angela. Nancy was their touchstone, their rudder, the one who loaded their lives and holiday tables with love, gingersnaps, and a dozen steaming dishes.

What would come of them?

"There are no words that will ease the pain of losing you," I told her. "But you have modeled strength your whole life. Your heart is as big as the ocean. Your legacy is love."

And so it went. The days of our visit melted together, like the fused art-glass plate. We turned on the ceiling fan, tucked our legs into the thick terrace cushions, and stared into the distance, watching a thousand glints of sunshine sparkle on the sea—such incongruous, poignant beauty.

We talked about our childhood, about the time I convinced her that she could feel African drumbeats all the way in Texas, if only she raised her hands into the air.

"Aha," I had shouted, back then, when I peeked around the corner to see her hands raised. "You believed me!"

Nancy's laughter, upon remembering that episode, felt as welcome as desert rain.

"I'm sorry," I said, "about teasing you so much when we were younger."

Nancy reached forward and patted my hand. "It's made for a great story for over fifty years."

I looked into her eyes, traveling farther inside than I ever had. We sat there, in utter silence, allowing the rawness of the inevitable to wash over us. Time and life were too precious to dwell on regrets.

Think about how we loved to laugh, she had written, and how easy it was to find beauty and humor when in each other's company.

In the midst of someone's sorrow and pain, I would tell my younger self, try to be one hundred percent present; don't back away. Even though you don't have a clue what to say or do, don't wilt in the face of inadequacy. Instead, in the midst of it, shine the light of who you are. Words are no match for grief, but another set of footprints, alongside yours, says, "I'm here, you're not alone. I'll walk this walk with you."

And when you lose someone, don't let the loss wipe out a lifetime of love and memories. Look in all of life's corners for the good times, fuse them together in your heart, think about being in each other's company, and let beauty and humor be the legacy of the person you loved.

Today, I walk to the hallway, lift Nancy's plate down from the shelf, and place my grilled cheese sandwich on top of it.

BONES

Heading north, into the wind, I push my way forward. The wind's bluster has excited the surf into a rough and pounding frenzy. The edge of my scarf snaps with each gust as bits of sea foam roll like tumbleweeds across the sand. Not many people have ventured out this morning, but I rather like the stirred-up energy of a storm and the waves thundering alongside me. The negative ions, stirred up by all the activity, invigorate me. They always have. Evidently, I am partial to negative ions, broken air molecules with more electrons than protons. Days like today coax me to walk five miles instead of my usual three.

The different moods of the sea mesmerize me—sometimes placidly reflecting the sky, mirror-like, other times rising from the ocean floor and hurling itself onto the shore, and still other times concealing dangerous riptides beneath benevolent waves. The same body of water encompasses it all; the sea is neither good nor bad. It just *is*. And, sometimes, on days like today, it coughs up bones.

A fourteen-inch-long bone, to be exact, weathe

white, wide as a bed slat. I pick it up, turning it over and over in my hand and brushing off the wet, gritty sand. I have never seen anything like it. Is it a dolphin bone? Could it be from a manatee? Surely not a whale. (It will be years before I know the answer.)

I carry the mystery bone home with me and clean it. It looks like bleached-white driftwood, quite lovely in fact. I add it to the shelf, visible beneath my glass-top kitchen table, nestling it among other bones of sorts, exoskeletons, all bleached salt-white by the sun: a sand dollar, a large chunk of coral, a starfish, and an angel's wing, a type of mollusk. These bones are relics, the beginnings and endings, of a life lived in the sea.

Someday, I, too, plan to become one with the sea. I wish to be cremated and my ashes scattered in the azure-blue waters of the Gulf, three nautical miles offshore, as mandated by the US Navy and Coast Guard. I like to think the words of Mary Frye's poem would bring some solace to those I leave behind: *Do not stand at my grave and weep. I am not there, I do not sleep. I am a thousand winds that blow; I am the diamond glints on snow . . . .*[9]

When the time comes, I will relinquish this faithful body of mine, and my soul, no longer encapsulated, will move on to wherever souls go. In my seventies, I am able to talk about my death with some equanimity; but my daughter, Mandy, finds this particular conversation painful. When she implores me to live at least a hundred years, I promise to try. Wanting to keep my promise, I have even taped a birthday card to the inside of my closet door, which says, "Celebrating 100 Wonderful Years!" I want my body to be inspired, too.

I hope I have ten thousand more beach walks ahead of me. But when my footprints no longer stand beside Mandy's in the sand, I want her to know I will be with her in a much larger sense. I pray she will hear my whispers in the surf, feel my love spread wide beneath the sky, and sense my abiding presence in leaping dolphins and soaring ospreys. When she sees sea foam skittering across the sand, I hope she pictures me dancing, completely free.

Become as vast as the sea, I would tell my younger self. The sea is big enough to hold everything—your joys and your sorrows, promises made and promises broken. Find beauty in the totality of life, its beginnings and even its endings. Don't shy away from the fullness of being. Life is neither good nor bad. It is sacred. No matter the weather, hold on to all of it: the storms, the calm, the beauty, even the riptides.

Let love be the bone of your being; that radiant, white essence that lives on, long after you are gone.

My slat of white bone no longer mystifies. I discovered it is a rib from a sea turtle. The bone's size indicates the turtle lived a long life. In mythologies throughout the world, sea turtles symbolize longevity, immortality, endurance, patience, and wisdom. I rather like being reminded of these things in the quiet of early morning, sipping my tea, the turtle bone and I, holding earthly vigil.

SHIFTING SHORELINES

Following on the heels of the full moon, the tide is low, like my mood.

My sister-friend Sue and I walk on hard-packed sand, eyes on the horizon, toward the north shore, where sand dollars bury themselves in shallow waters. The whole north end was reshaped by Hurricane Irma, which made landfall less than four months ago with wind speeds of 130 miles per hour. Blue tarps still dot a few rooftops, a spattering of chickee huts wait to be rethatched, and numerous palm trees appear undecided about sending forth new palm fronds. The hurricane carried away 128 million gallons of sand in our surrounding area, changing miles of shoreline.[10]

But Irma's impact didn't stop there.

Irma also changed the shoreline of my life. Sue, who has been Thelma to my Louise for thirty-plus years, was supposed to grow old with me on this small island. Sue, who regularly walks the beach with me; who gave me a sun parasol because we joked about becoming *umbrella ladies*; who once tied her friendship thread to mine before we tossed them into this very sea; who joins me in visits to the statue of Margo, our island mermaid; who laughs, cries, and celebrates life's milestones with me, is moving. The evacuation, before Irma struck, was such an ordeal for Sue and her family that they decided to move to North Carolina, far enough inland to avoid any future hurricanes— far enough inland, and away, to change the landscape of our lives.

Reorienting will be a process, like repairing torn rooftops and waiting for new growth on stripped trees. I will be fine; I know that. Sue will be fine, too. But our walk is more somber today, quieter and more poignant. We are walking toward our favorite lunch spot for one last lunch before she leaves. Over fish tacos, we try to convince ourselves and each other that 850 miles will not make that much of a difference . . . surely. We vow to try and see each other at least twice a year.

We reminisce about leading trips together, weaving laurel sprigs into head garlands in Greece, listening for our secret names while floating in the sea, making masks of our faces, buying identical osprey friendship rings, and folding onto the floor in laughter when we worked on our business expenses and had to call upon *woodman*, a grade school math mnemonic, to figure out simple addition. So many shared memories and experiences bind us. Surely, glue like this can withstand 850 miles.

After paying our bill, we visit Margo the mermaid, a seagreen sculpture, gilded in gold, which has welcomed island visitors for more than half a century. Margo's tail curves around a base, and she extends one hand that holds a conch shell. Margo has become our shared symbol for the deep feminine, that which is born from the sea, the unconscious. Eyes closed, fingers touching, Sue and I cup our hands over Margo's hand; we offer gratitude for all that has been and for all that is yet to be.

We meander back, past familiar places, the spot where we once left flowers, the spot where we wrote messages in the sand. I point to another place. "That's where we moved the grand piano." We both laugh, remembering her dream about a grand piano that was out of place in her dream bedroom. It was not uncommon for us to honor our dreams by writing them down, discussing them, and, sometimes, even enacting some portion of them, which is why we decided to pretend to carry an imaginary grand piano out of her bedroom for the simple fact it did not belong there.

I look down at the water's edge to see a double sunray Venus shell gleaming in the sun. A Venus bivalve is a single shell with two identical sides; when splayed open, the two sides look like the striated wings of a butterfly. Anne Morrow Lindbergh wrote about a sunray bivalve in her book *Gift From the Sea*. It was about relationships.

> *One learns to accept the fact that no permanent return is possible to an old form of relationship; and, more deeply still, that there is no holding of a relationship to a single form. This is not tragedy but part of the ever-recurrent miracle of life and growth. All living relationships are in process of change, of expansion, and must perpetually be building themselves new forms.*[11]

"This is a symbol of our friendship," I say, bending to pick up the shell, gently pulling it apart, and handing Sue half of it. "We'll each have a half of a whole."

Sue cups her palm tenderly around the shell. "I'll keep mine on my desk," she says.

"I'll do the same," I answer.

We pause outside the beach gate, leaving other treasures we found on a nearby rock—a feather, more shells, and a thin piece of string we knotted together.

This is how we say goodbye . . . one last glance around, on the new shoreline of our friendship.

Shorelines are seldom permanent, I would tell my younger self. Tides and storms wash in and out. Nothing is forever, except change. Change may be our most permanent commodity. It's okay to dream, plan, and build, but do it knowing that the winds of change will surely visit you. They may be gentle tides and winds, slowly sculpting a new shoreline, or violent storms that totally rearrange the landscape. Either way, you are built to withstand the changing shorelines of your life. Clasp your hand around that which arises from deep within you. Offer gratitude for what you have and ask blessings on all that is yet to be.

And when you find a friend, cherish her; offer her the keys to your heart, buy her a parasol, discover each other's secret name, walk the changing shoreline together, and, most of all, be sure to tend your half of the whole.

Later, I take out my binoculars. I can still see the other shells we gathered and left, as well as the feather Sue placed on a rock beside the beach gate. Fishing out a felt pen from the kitchen drawer, I write *BFF* on my half of the sunray Venus. I carry it gingerly into my office and pause before the bookshelf where the *singing twins* rest. I love this figurine of two Native American women joined in such a way as to form only one lap, their faces uplifted as they sing. Sue and I have passed this figurine between us, every six months, for almost twenty years.

I place my shell there, between them, in the lap of friendship.

MOON CALENDAR

I move the dial on my moon calendar exactly one shell forward—from the angel wing, aptly named, toward the sea biscuit, resembling a fluffed-up sand dollar. This means nothing to the untrained eye, but, to me, the creator of this circular, three-dimensional moon calendar, it means we are four days away from the new moon, the time each month the moon disappears into a tomb of darkness. Three days later, when my dial points toward a curved, white spiral, called a baby's ear, I know the western sky will give birth to a new crescent moon at twilight.

I never tire of the moon's shape-shifting, most especially when the crescent moon appears to cradle the *old moon* in her arms. Most everyone, including Leonardo da Vinci, has witnessed this phenomenon: when the ghostly outline of the old moon's dark surface can be seen nestled inside the bright white arms of the new crescent. The crescent, like a bedazzled young woman, cradles the old moon, a dark-cloaked grandmother, seemingly lit by candlelight. Leonardo da Vinci described the ashen candlelight as a *ghostly glow* caused by sunlight reflecting off the earth, more commonly known as earthshine.

Da Vinci's codex of drawings, descriptions, and calculations of the moon's phases is much more scientific than mine. My moon calendar, created almost a decade ago, lives inside an old, wide-mouthed pottery bowl that I found in an antique store in Greece. Filling the earth-colored bowl with sand, I circled twenty-nine small specimen shells from my collection along the inside perimeter of the bowl, to correspond to the approximate 29.5 days between full moons. In the very center of the bowl, I positioned a movable wooden spinner that I manually turn every day. It very much resembles a clock. When the dial points upward, in the twelve o'clock position, it points to a fanned scallop shell, the largest of my twenty-nine shells; it represents the full moon. The first quarter phase, at three o'clock, is marked by a scotch bonnet; the new moon, at six o'clock, by a small sand dollar; and the last quarter, at nine o'clock, by a spiny jewel box. The waxing and waning gibbous phases of each day are represented by eighteen different varieties of shells.

This daily ritual attunes me to the phases of the moon, which orchestrate the rising and falling tides. I know when the full moon will rise in the east and when the waxing crescent will set in the west. I am like the tides; the moon has always tugged on my psyche. Even as a child, I remember marveling when moonlight streamed into my bedroom window, turning every ordinary object in the room into something luminous. Nothing looked shabby cloaked in moonlight. As an adolescent, I even wrote a poem about an old woman, who, every full moon, took a moon bath. For a few short hours, she became young again.

Beneath the Moon

Her crepe skin smoothed to lucent porcelain;
Wisps of gray gleamed raven black.
Moonlight revealed her youth,
Dormant,
Beneath the layered dust of years.

I had forgotten about her until one night, not that long ago, when I stepped naked onto my private, moon-splashed balcony, overlooking the sea. The moonlight, so beautiful and bright, enveloped me in liquid satin. Turning my face upward toward the face of the moon, listening to the whispering surf, and feeling the cool breeze against my skin, I remembered the old woman in my story taking a moon bath . . . .

And here she was, all these years later. She was me.

If I had known back then, I would have added one last line to my poem: The moon, dazzling the night and shimmering upon the sea, illuminated the old woman's dancing body and set her free.

Dance. Dance often, I would tell my younger self. And you must, at least once, dance naked beneath a full moon. Don't look so shocked, I would add. It's good for the soul, especially an old soul. Your body is your soul's holy temple. Lift open its latch and set your vastness free. Don't clip your wings. Dance to the music of the moon.

Track the moon's wanings and waxings; they parallel the wanings and waxings of life. Sometimes life is about new beginnings, bright prospects, new projects; it's a burgeoning phase full of promise and light. And sometimes, life is about endings, dimming hopes, and being asked to sit in a dark place void of light. Rest in this dark place, and know that light will come again. Nothing is static. The dial keeps turning, wanings and waxings, scallop to sand dollar, scotch bonnet to spiny jewel box, all inside this great bowl of life.

I trace my finger across the rough rim of my moon-bowl calendar. The new moon crescent now holds another meaning for me. In addition to holding the old moon in her arms, she will hold me, a dancing old woman, reflecting the earthshine of her years.

SAND WRITINGS

The sea is a good listener. Maybe this is why people trouble to find a shell or piece of driftwood and bend to etch a message on its shore. Each message, carved into the soft flesh of tide-washed sand, reminds me of a Rorschach, revealing what lies within the heart at that very moment. I call these messages *sand writings*, and I often pause to read them, wondering about the lives of the people who authored them.

Who are they, I wonder? Are they young, old, madly in love, or looking for love? Is this their first visit to this island, or have they, like me, been walking this beach for decades?

One thing seems certain. We all are drawn to the sea.

I'm strolling south, now, toward one of these sand writings. I noticed it yesterday from my kitchen window, but I couldn't make out the words, even with the binoculars, which I keep within an arm's reach of the window. I am most curious as to why the morning beach plow has spared it. I often watch the plow humming along the shore, raking the sand smooth and readying our strand of beach for another day. Occasionally, the plow spares a particularly exceptional sandcastle, but I have never seen it curve a clawed path around a sand writing.

It did the same today; that's two days in a row.

I have put off practicing my harp to see why the plow did this. Plus, taking a walk for whatever reason is medicine for my soul. A morning walk beneath the spectacle of sky, painted with the brushstrokes of dawn, is like a tuning key for the psyche.

I happen to know a little about tuning keys. I bought one last year along with a Celtic harp. Long an admirer, the idea to actually buy a harp was ignited during a visit to the Old Library of Trinity College in Dublin. As I stood admiring an encased, exquisitely carved eight-hundred-year-old harp in the book-laden shelves of the Long Room, I decided, then and there, to join the bards and take harp lessons.

Unfortunately, a bard I will never be.

I am much better at harp tuning, twisting my tuning key to sharpen or flatten a harp string until the tuner's needle hovers in the green zone. Translating the hieroglyphic black notes in my music book into a song on my twenty-six-string harp often eludes me. Still, I persevere, but only because I have reframed my efforts.

Instead of referring to my lessons as *harp practice*, I now call them *harp prayer*. Instead of fretting about proficiency, I focus on intention. This new paradigm allows me to imagine that each plucked quivering harp string, no matter how off-key or off-tempo, releases a vibration of love and prayer into the world. It's the least I can do, actually, for all that has been given me. Which is why, when I return from this walk, I will wrap my arms about my harp and pray for a while.

I have come, now, to the place where the morning plow curved around the sand writing. I stop to read the etched words in the sand. They are not the usual fare of love initials, or a birthday wish, or where someone is from. I see why the driver curved carefully around the words. They strike a profound chord of loss.

WE MISS
YOU CORY
DADDY <3

I stand there, quietly absorbing the grief in the words, wondering whose hand authored them—most likely a father, grieving his lost child. Whatever the case, this sandy epitaph cuts deeply. I am struck by the glorious sunrise juxtaposed against this sorrow and loss. How can the human heart reconcile such opposites?

I am no stranger to grief. Few of us are. Recently, I lost my adult sister to pancreatic cancer, my young, vibrant brother-in-law to a raging infection, and, years before that, my twelve-year-old brother to brain cancer, my two-year-old brother to an accidental overdose of my mother's sleeping pills, my mother to a drug overdose when she was forty, and my biological father to a self-inflicted gunshot wound.

I rarely pour all of these losses into a single cup, but, this morning, here they are, spilling over the sides, as I imagine a dad writing a note to his lost son. I can picture Cory's dad at the edge of the shore, his silhouette bending and rising, as he lays bare the words of his heart, etched into the sand.

The sea listens, the sky brightens, and the driver of a morning plow pays his respects.

What I have learned about loss, I would tell my younger self, is that you really never lose it. It will be with you always, sometimes quietly tucked away in the background, sometimes stomach-punching present in the foreground. Loss breaks us open, and the only way to absorb it is to allow it to take up residence inside us, let it howl at times, give it permission to carve new hollows, but never let it permanently exclude joy. This is why we must grow and expand—no matter how painful the hollowing and expansion might be.

Dynamite whatever bedrock needed to find a place to hold your losses, but never evict joy. It is possible for loss and joy to dwell together in the same heart; they can live on the same street. And, if ever invited in, joy can sometimes fill the hollows loss carves. Savor every beautiful moment you experience—your pink sunrises, your walks along the shoreline, your daughter hugging your neck, your cats purring on your lap, your husband giving you a thumbs-up, your sisters' laughter, everything that causes you to sigh and ache. For that ache is where joy and sorrow meet.

After my walk, I retrieve my harp from its stand and cradle it between my knees. Bracketing my fingers on the strings C, E, and G, I begin to play "Morning Has Broken." I imagine my halting notes are prayers, filling hollowed places. I pray for the people in my life who are struggling and hurting; I pray for the people who are gone; I pray for the world's brokenness; and, today, most especially, today, I pray for Cory's grief-stricken family.

JUDAS SNAKE

It was only a matter of time.

And, evidently, that time has come.

"If there's one of them, there's going to be up to forty," said a python hunter who captured a live, six-foot Burmese python on our island. While holding the two-year-old python, coiled snugly about his wrist, the hunter added that the snake surely had "brothers and sisters" in the area.[12] In fact, there could be up to one hundred brothers and sisters—the number of eggs a female python can lay in a single clutch.

Generally, my philosophy is *live and let live*. I respect all wildlife, even snakes. I have always been rather fascinated with serpents and have visited several serpentariums over the years. Much to my husband's chagrin, I have even held a python during an educational presentation. I have a corporeal memory of the snake's weighty underbelly, dry and smooth, almost rubberlike against my arms. But I admit to liking pythons that hang out in enclosures, or the jungle, much more than the pythons invading southwest Florida.

My live-and-let-live policy comes into question with invasive species. Burmese pythons are not native to southwest Florida; in fact, their numbers have burgeoned to such a degree that they are decimating wildlife and wreaking havoc on native species. Some pythons can even eat alligators. According to the United States Geological Survey, Burmese pythons are "one of the most concerning invasive species in Everglades National Park." In one region of the park, "populations of raccoons . . . dropped 99.3 percent, opossums 98.9 percent, and bobcats 87.5 percent." Plus, other wildlife—foxes, marsh rabbits, and cottontail rabbits—have basically disappeared.[13]

Because of these staggering statistics, southwest Florida has instituted programs to eliminate pythons from the region. Together, the python elimination programs, which include sanctioned hunts, a yearly event called the Python Bowl, and paid bounties (fifty dollars for snakes up to four feet long and an additional twenty-five dollars for every foot thereafter) have, in the last three years, humanely euthanized pythons whose combined weight exceeds an astonishing thirty-six thousand pounds.[14]

However, it's estimated there are tens of thousands of pythons in the wild.[15] Eradicating them will be virtually impossible. They are not only invasive; they are evasive. The python's sun-speckled diamond pattern camouflages it so effectively that a person could be within a foot of one in the underbrush and not know it. In addition, Florida pythons have no enemies, except for the hunters who garner hourly wages hunting them.

Patti, a friend of mine, attended a training to capture pythons. While I'm sure it would be fascinating to watch the capture of a writhing python, I have no desire to wrestle up to fifty pounds of snake, grab it with both hands behind its head, and attempt to stuff five or six uncooperative feet of it into a cloth bag. Patti is a hardy type, once inviting me to take a swamp walk with her, saying, as an aside, the water should only be thigh-high. I double-checked to make sure she wasn't joking. She wasn't. She said they only walked in daylight so they could spot water moccasins and gators. Although she informed me that gators are easily seen at night, if you shine a light into their eyes, but she didn't fancy night walks. I explained that my idea of a walk usually mandated dry ground, and I did not fancy close encounters with alligators, water moccasins, or pythons.

The only invitations I have accepted from Patti, thus far, are lunch dates and a benign python lecture at the zoo, where I saw a jaw-dropping slide of five people holding a euthanized female Burmese python, eighteen feet long, weighing 133 pounds, caught south of us.

During the presentation, I learned that female Burmese pythons comprise the greatest threat because of their capability to lay such a large clutch of eggs every year. "This," our lecturer said, "has given rise to Judas snakes." My ears perked up. *Judas snakes*? Whatever could they be?

Judas snakes are equipped with tracking devices. Instead of euthanizing all male pythons, some are surgically implanted with a radio transmitter, tagged, and released back into the wild. The movements of these pythons help researchers learn more about their range, habits, and breeding areas. The name *Judas* comes from what is termed a *betrayal event*. The males, seeking to mate, sometimes lead python hunters to the females, betraying not only the location of the female python but also the location of other males, sometimes numbering up to five, who are also attracted to the female during their five-month breeding season.

I have to admit, when I'm kayaking, I keep a watchful eye near the water's edge of the densely vegetated mangrove islands (for pythons can swim short distances). If pythons have migrated to our populated island with limited wildlife, they surely have discovered our nearby uninhabited islands. I am clear that I would not, under any circumstances, wrestle a python. However, I would report it.

I've downloaded the IveGot1 app, which reports sightings. Should I ever see a python, I, too, will become a Judas of sorts, simply by clicking the Burmese python link. The app automatically records the time, longitude, and latitude and provides a place to download a photo, should I take one.

These are not perfect systems, but they are proving to be effective ways of tracking down pythons. Left unchecked, much of southwest Florida's ecosystem could collapse.

Invasive species, I would tell my younger self, are things that threaten your equilibrium, threaten to destroy your well-being, or threaten to swallow up your joy. Invasive species can invade your inner world as well as your outer world. Internally, they might be camouflaged as a desire to be perfect or to please, or they may be experienced as paralyzing self-doubt, worry, and negative self-talk. Invasive species, whether they be habits or thoughts, sap vital creative energy and upset balance and harmony. Identify and ferret out these influences as best you can. Left unchecked, these things have the power to seize, strangle, and destroy well-being and confidence.

And if an invasive species comes from outside you in the guise of unsupportive friends or family members, or limiting societal roles and expectations, there's no need to engage. Assess, recognize you've got one (or more), and paddle away—if not physically, then psychologically. Do not allow some foreign energy to wreak havoc in your life. Take steps to eradicate or mitigate that which fosters imbalance. Joy is too precious to be devoured by unwelcome predators.

As I finish writing this, I realize I need to be in touch with Patti; I promised we would get together soon. She may be thinking swamp hikes and python bags, but I have something tamer in mind: maybe a Caesar salad and iced tea.

BROKEN

Oh, no!

My half of the sunray Venus clamshell—the shell I found when Sue and I said goodbye, the shell I unhinged and said, "This is a symbol of our friendship; we'll each have a half of the whole"—lies broken into three pieces on top of my desk.

An uncensored thought flashes through my mind. Could the broken shell portend something amiss with our friendship?

How can you think that? I scold myself. But I know the origins of such thinking.

In my younger years, when I moved away from friends, distance often reshaped the shoreline of those friendships— not because anyone wished it to be so but because miles, different time zones, and new routines eroded the familiar edges of what used to be. I puzzled why some of my long-distance friendships fell by the wayside while others persisted.

I have come to understand the difference between reshaping and erosion. The erosion of some friendships was due to proximity—miles did make a difference. But with other friends, miles do not matter. Distance may reshape how often we see one another, but it has little bearing on how much we love one another.

I am confident this will be true for me and Sue; we have so much history. My rational self knows that my clamshell was merely dropped, accidentally, from the shelf onto my desk by either a guest or a housekeeper. Dropping it might seem inconsequential or entirely forgettable to someone else. There are, after all, thousands of other shells on the beach right outside my window. No one could guess the sentimental value I have assigned to this shell, except, perhaps, Sue, who has the matching half. But despite my rational thinking, some part of myself still fears that no one is immune to erosion.

The broken pieces clack together as I turn them over in my hand. The initials *BFF* remain intact. I printed them inside the shell right after our lunch that afternoon, five months earlier, just before she moved.

I don't want the broken shell to be a portent of something fracturing between us.

Not long ago, I dreamed I was walking along the sidewalk and excitedly recognized Sue sitting on the porch of her new home, 850 miles away. Before I could call out to her, I realized (in my dream) that she was busy and would not welcome a visit. Sadly, I hung my head and walked on by, without waving or saying a word—something that would never happen in waking life.

I have worked with dreams, mine and others, for over

thirty years. Using symbolism and imagery, dreams attempt to bring more conscious awareness to our psyche; their messages are often nuanced and multilayered. But I have no doubt that one layer of my dream speaks to my sadness over losing the close proximity to Sue. She has adjusted quite nicely in her new location; she's busy meeting new people, discovering new places, and working on a writing project. I am happy for her, of course, but I still feel the empty spaces she left behind; I miss our heartfelt talks, easy laughter, and timeless lunches.

At first, I tried to tamp down my feelings, rationalizing that I shouldn't feel sad and telling myself that all is for the best, which, indeed, may be true. But, recently, I have allowed myself to feel my feelings more honestly. Instead of battening down the hatches to my heart, I am throwing open the shutters, hoping my feelings will move in and through me, like one of our fast-moving rainstorms, riding the northwest wind.

In essence, I am allowing myself to feel the empty pockets of our friendship; I am allowing myself to miss her; I am allowing myself to feel a little broken. I am reshaping.

The best way to deal with your feelings, I would tell my younger self, is simply to allow yourself to feel them. Don't bury your feelings in the unconscious, where they may smolder and erupt later, like molten lava. Just as you are unable to control yourself from feeling heat, cold, or pain, the same is true for feelings. They are temperatures of the psyche; they are a response.

You can't control your feelings, but you can control what you do with your feelings. Feel them, instead of acting them out. Observe them.

Weather them, like weather patterns moving across the sky of your mind. Just as you are not the weather, neither are you your feelings. They are not the totality of who you are. Which is why, if you or a friend moves away, you can be happy and still feel sad. It's okay. It means you really care. Take heart in knowing that deep, abiding friendships have a way of weathering time and distance.

Also, keep in mind, it is often harder to be left than to leave. When someone leaves you, there is an empty space where they used to be; it takes a while for the tide of time to fill in those spaces. Be patient, new frontiers await. Remember the words of English mystic and theologian Julian of Norwich: "All shall be well, and all shall be well, and all manner of things shall be well."

I rummage through the kitchen cabinet for a toothpick, search the hardware cabinet for glue, and spread out the broken pieces of the shell onto a piece of wax paper.

The metaphor of tending is not lost on me.

MERMAID TEARS

Today, of all days, I find a tear. It seems fitting.

Those of us living entwined lives with the sea likely possess a few mermaid tears. Mine are frosted green. I found yet another one this morning, a trapezoid about the size of a dime, which looks very much like crystallized seawater. No wonder sailors of old often called these tumbled pieces of sea glass mermaid tears, guessing their translucent quality originated from luminescent tears, cried beneath the waves, instead of broken shards of glass.

The folklore surrounding mermaid tears is as colorful as sea glass itself. Some lore says mermaids wept whenever a sailor drowned at sea. Another myth tells the story of a particular mermaid who, defying Neptune, intervened in human affairs by calming the winds and waves to protect a captain she loved. Upon hearing of this transgression, wrathful Neptune brandished his trident and forever banished the weeping mermaid to the bottom of the sea, never to see her captain again.

Sea glass begs for an origin story—even in the twenty-first century. I cannot help but wonder about each piece. Is it a piece of shipwrecked treasure or litter, tossed into the sea? What was it before: A glass, a bottle, or something more exotic like a Venetian chandelier? What is its story? How long has it been in the sea?

Some surmise it can take twenty to fifty years of churning to render a broken shard into a smoothed-edged piece of sea glass.[16] I run my fingers across the minuscule pits of the glass in my hand; the velvety feel comes from soda and lime leaching out of the glass. I cannot guess its age. I only know the more like velvet it feels, the longer it has been in the sea.

Rough seas can smooth sharp edges. Life and adversity can do that, too.

I think of my grandparents living on a farm, surviving the Great Depression, drought, and blights of pests. They met whatever befell them; they brushed dirt from their knees, planted more crops, and continued on. They personified the patina of aged sea glass—tumbled, leached, and smoothed—not only in their psyche but physically, as well. I remember sitting for hours, stroking my grandma's smooth, wise, time-worn hands.

Today, however, I feel more like a razor-sharp shard than smoothed sea glass—hope leaches from my pores.

This week, a little more than a hundred miles away, a troubled teenager stole into a Parkland, Florida, high school with a legally purchased AR-15 rifle. Within seven minutes, he killed seventeen students and faculty and wounded seventeen others. This absolutely shattering news brought me to my knees. These numbers, along with those from Columbine, Sandy Hook, and too many others, are not statistics; they are flesh-and-blood lives. They belong to children who once sat in their grandparent's lap, children who will never graduate, children who just happened to be in the crosshairs of an assault rifle in their classroom.

There are not enough tears.

In the aftermath of Parkland, thousands of students rallied at the state capitol and in Washington, pleading, amid their tears, for tougher gun laws.

Sadly, the sale of AR-15s spiked right after the shooting.[17] So, too, did the sale of bulletproof backpacks.[18] Worried parents are purchasing bulletproof backpacks—praying that when they kiss their daughter or son goodbye in the morning, they will also be able to kiss them good night in the evening.

How have we, as a society, sunk to the point that bulletproof backpacks can be considered a back-to-school purchase? Surely a banished archetypal feminine weeps for us and our children. What wrathful Neptune, in our midst, brandishes his trident, forbidding our intervention to save the lives of those we love? I mourn the banishment of this defiant feminine archetype, buried in our collective unconscious, at the bottom of the sea.

She cries her tears, and I cry mine.

But what can I, a seventy-year-old woman, do?

When your heart is broken open, I would tell my younger self, and ragged tears slide down your cheeks, tumble them in your heart. Crystallize them into gems of compassion and action, reflecting your individual color of caring, however it manifests. Let your tears rise from the depths of despair and wash onto the shore of collective consciousness. Write a letter, speak out, or demonstrate. Take the shipwrecked litter of life and turn it into something good, strong, and beautiful. Don't let the weeping of the deep feminine be cried in vain. Create a new myth, defy the brandishing trident of unlimited power, magnify love—the luminescence inside many a tear.

After my walk, I light a candle, gather my mermaid tears around me, and begin a letter.

Dear Senator . . .

PALEO & CALUSA

Last week, an eagle, its mighty talons poised to snatch a fish from the sea, swooped so close to the shore that I saw the gold of its eye.

I pull off the road now, not far from the beach, park on the worn grass, and seat myself on the sun-warmed observation bench. An eagle, known on our island as Calusa, perches near her giant nest, an aerie, which resembles a stack of kindling large enough for a bonfire; unbelievably, the nest probably weighs close to a thousand pounds. The largest recorded bald eagle nest, located about three hours north of us, weighed almost six thousand pounds.[19]

Calusa's bone-white head feathers gleam in the sunlight as she scans the horizon. I surmise she's looking for her mate, Paleo. My heart is heavy for her; the news of Paleo's unfortunate accident spread quickly through the island.

For at least twelve years, each fall, Calusa and Paleo, a pair of American bald eagles named by local elementary children for the indigenous people of our island, have returned to these 11.6 acres, designated as a nature preserve and bird sanctuary. Upon their arrival, the eagles painstakingly repair and rebuild their nest in the towering Australian pine before me, although this year the pine's limbs have been thinned considerably by Hurricane Irma.

The surrounding homeowners, abutting this wild, undeveloped tract of land, sometimes cut and stack mango branches at the edge of their property, hoping the pair will snatch a branch for their treetop home. Some have observed the birds picking up a branch in their beak, tossing it into the air, and catching it with their talons before flying to the nest. Looking through a telescope, one observer commented that the eagles do not always agree on their remodeling efforts. If one tries to rearrange a branch, the other might place a talon on it, indicating it's fine where it is.

Through the years, Paleo and Calusa have faced hardships, like storms and illegal fireworks set off on New Year's Eve. Two years in a row, the fireworks scared the pair away from their nest, causing them to abandon their clutch of eggs. This year, thankfully, there were no fireworks. Calusa laid two eggs; she and Paleo have been raising and feeding their two fuzzy fledglings, now occupying the nest.

This long-awaited eagle foursome makes last night's accident all the more heart-rending.

Paleo, evidently misjudging his six-foot wingspan, electrocuted himself on a nearby power line, leaving behind his life mate and baby chicks. His lifeless, magnificent body was found on the ground below. With his demise, raising and feeding the fledglings will fall solely to Calusa, not an easy task.

I sigh, wondering if she is up to the challenge.

The Calusa Indians, a Paleo-Indian tribe for which the

eagle pair was named, inhabited this island for more than a thousand years. The Calusa were accomplished artisans and fishermen, but they were also fierce warriors. I think about fierceness. We use it to describe a mother's love for her child. I have experienced that fierce, instinctual drive to keep your child safe.

Once, when Mandy and I were watching a meteor shower with others in a darkened field, we were separated. The moment I realized my nine-year-old daughter was not by my side, I experienced a frenzied flurry of adrenaline so forceful that I will never forget it. I blindly ripped through the cornstalks shouting Mandy's name, ready to do battle with whatever or whomever dared to come between me and my child. I am five feet, five inches tall, but that night my fierceness towered toward the stars raining down all around me. When I heard Mandy's voice say, "I'm over here, Mommy," and learned she was watching a train, my fierceness melted into tears.

Calusa will need to be fierce. I send her goodwill as she spreads her magnificent wings and swoops to the nest. The downy heads of her eaglets bob slightly above the aerie's edge.

Even though we live by the rules, I would tell my younger self, life may not unfold the way we plan. Unforeseen circumstances may rob us of our peace of mind, our health, our opportunities, even our loved ones. We may be asked to shoulder a responsibility alone or carry on an endeavor by ourselves; it takes a fierce will to stare hardship in the eye. Fierceness calls forth reserves from the soul. Refuse to be hardened by hardship. Cling to the belief that, if called upon, your fierceness can tower toward the stars.

And when hardship comes, as it's bound to do, remember you may not be as alone as you imagine. There could be others in the wings, watching, hurting, hoping, caring, cheering, and sending healing prayers your way.

Days later, I hear more travails about Calusa. A rogue male eagle tossed the eaglets from their nest after Calusa dropped off a fish for their dinner. Upon returning, she chased the male eagle away, but the chicks remained stranded on the ground. Thankfully, the Conservancy of Southwest Florida stepped in to rescue the eaglets, but it was deemed too dangerous to return them to the nest, where they might be ousted again. Instead, they are being cared for until they are old enough to be released into the wild on their own.

Calusa, a bit bewildered, I imagine, has flown away.

I'm not the only one who will be watching and waiting for her this coming September. Will she return to the same nest with a new mate? Time will tell.

May her fierce determination prevail.★

★Calusa returned to the nest the following year and did, indeed, find a new mate. Local fifth graders voted to name the new male Herb, in memory of a prominent island architect who died five days short of his one hundredth birthday. Calusa and Herb raised two healthy eaglets their first year together.

RED TIDE

Still groggy and desiring some cheerfulness along with my morning tea, I switch on the miniature lights woven throughout my Christmas village. I call my village, which I painstakingly erect every Christmas, Utopia. I explain to those who are curious that nothing bad ever happens in Utopia. Peace and well-being blanket the village like new-fallen snow. The children, throwing snow-balls and ice skating on the pond, have no worries or fears in Utopia; the neighbors, carolers, and shopkeepers look out for one another; the cats and dogs live in warm, loving homes; and the trusty lamplighter lights the glowing lamps each evening.

I sometimes imagine myself walking down the cobble-stone streets in Utopia, free of worry and fear. Oftentimes an ache of longing sweeps through me, making me home-sick for such a world, as if I'm lost and trying to find my way home. On the highest village hill, I have positioned an angel that my sister Vicki gave me. I named her the Guard-ian Angel of Utopia. She holds a banner of peace between her hands; I like to think she welcomes prayers and inquiries from this world as well.

After finishing my imaginary stroll in Utopia, I walk into the kitchen, where Jim sits reading on his phone. I throw open the slider door and inhale deeply, expecting my lungs to fill with fresh salt air. I cough instead.

Oh, no. Not again.

My Utopian mood bursts. I don't smell anything, but I feel the familiar catch in the back of my throat.

Maybe it's just coincidence.

I inhale again. And, again, I cough. It's not coincidence. There are toxins in the air; I'm sure of it.

Our north wind, like the conch-carrying wind god Boreas, brings less humidity and cooler temperatures in the winter. I greet these welcome northerly breezes by throwing open our glass sliding doors, unfurling a soft blanket at night, and snuggling down to listen to the louder-than-normal surf, eventually drifting into a deep sleep. One culprit, however, can wreak havoc on this coveted time of year.

Occasionally, the north wind escorts an unwelcome, hazardous visitor to our doorstep: red tide. An algal bloom of *Karenia brevis*, red tide occurs naturally in the Gulf of Mexico, but sometimes the blooms reach harmful levels. No one knows the exact causes for the severity of these outbreaks, but several precursors likely collide. Many contend that the runoff from fertilizers (applied to the myriad of lawns, golf courses, and fields in our region) increases the frequency and duration of a red-tide outbreak; fertilizers' nitrogen and phosphorus compounds cause algae to reproduce rapidly. Global warming may also be a player.

In any case, I appear to be a human red-tide barometer,

even at low levels. I feel a hair-like tickle, deep in my throat, just above my Adam's apple. Then the cough comes—a dry, persistent cough, caused by the release of brevetoxins when the algal blooms break apart in the wave and surf action. The toxins aerosolize in the sea spray.

"We have red tide," I tell Jim, who is still sitting at the breakfast table. He peers at me over the top of his reading glasses, not quite convinced. He is rarely bothered by the outbreaks. He holds up his phone, checks our county-wide red-tide hotline, which details the levels of red tide in our area, and raises his eyebrows, a sure sign that I am correct.

My ways of knowing baffle him sometimes, in a good way, I think. He is more logical, needing the confirmation of tangible charts and hotlines; I am more intuitive, depending on my interactions with the environment around me. In the early years of our marriage, I felt our differences more sharply. Both of us can be headstrong. However, time and patience have smoothed away many of those sharp edges and proved to me that, together, we make a solid pair.

However, this morning, I would prefer not to be right.

Jim reads the caution issued for people with chronic respiratory issues: they should avoid the beach until levels decline. I begrudgingly close our glass slider. Even though I don't have health issues, I will avoid the beach until the algal blooms push offshore. I can't breathe without incessantly coughing when the red-tide levels are this high.

Unfortunately, manatees, turtles, fish, and dolphins have no protective windows or doors to close, nor can they avoid the sea. The same toxins that cause respiratory irritation in humans can also kill marine life when breathed and ingested.

I remember a particularly bad outbreak of red tide some years earlier, in 1996; thousands of dead fish floated lifelessly on top of the water, and the beach lay littered for miles with fish carcasses that washed ashore. It saddened me to learn that 238 manatees died that year, nearly ten percent of our endangered manatee population.[20] The air quality on the beach was so compromised that I had to drive off-island just to breathe fresh air.

Reluctantly, I have come to accept these outbreaks as part of a natural rhythm. Certainly, if fertilizers exacerbate the problem, then limits need to be set to protect our marine life. But red tide, itself, is a natural phenomenon in the Gulf, documented since the mid-1800s. Red tide, like mosquitoes and hurricanes, reveals the underside of paradise, a price exacted for sunshine, palm trees, and ocean breezes.

As badly as I long for it, there is no Utopia in this world, not even in paradise. I will forever be an optimist, but I try not to be a Pollyanna, either. It is difficult, at times, to walk the fine line between the two. In truth, if I err, I want it to be on the side of optimism. Pessimism and cynicism are toxic visitors as unwelcome in my world as red tide.

There is no Utopia, I would tell my younger self, not in this world. The closest you will come to it is your Christmas village. Every year you will add to it: a bench here, a tree there. Even though your Utopia is make-believe, it will be worth the hours you labor to bring it into being. Wonder will shine in the eyes of children and adults as they study the miniature scenes lining the length of your credenza, from the deer edging out of the pine forest all the way to the train station on the other side of town. There are no locked doors in your snow-covered Utopia, no disease, no political divides, and, certainly, no red tide—only a quiet blanket of calm, peace, and well-being.

It does the heart good to seed these feelings in others and the world. But don't let your well-being and joy depend upon nothing bad ever happening. Every paradise has its underbelly, every relationship a sore spot, every sunny day a shadow. Try to weather these inevitabilities without succumbing to pessimism or cynicism. Wait for the winds to change, tuck in, protect yourself from that which is toxic, and celebrate and magnify the goodness and beauty surrounding you (even if it takes hours). Sow beauty and reap gratitude.

There's something else, too. Don't forget to give thanks for the bespectacled husband, baffled by your ways, sitting across from you at the kitchen table.

"Want to go on a boondoggle?" I ask Jim, my code for spending the afternoon out.

"Doing what?" he asks, tidying up.

I tilt up the kitchen shutters, helping to block the sun and keep things cool while we are gone. "I don't know. Maybe do some Christmas shopping, run some errands, and have lunch off the island. Maybe Steamers?"

Within the hour, we are driving over the bridge, off the island, leaving paradise (and its underbelly) behind for the afternoon.

PANDEMIC

"What day is it?" I ask Jim as I use my elbow to clink the beach gate closed behind us, my toes sinking into a foot of new, sugar-soft sand.

"Tuesday," Jim answers, tucking the gate key into his pocket. "No, it's Wednesday," he says more decisively.

Our days have become indistinguishable, except for the COVID-19 numbers, which keep climbing: two hundred thousand[†] cases today in the United States, more than both China and Italy combined.

Backdropped against this worldwide pandemic, a dredge ship hums surreally in the channel south of us, raking the bottom of the Gulf like a giant cheese grater, vacuuming up accumulated sand that threatens to make the boat channel impassable. We, on the south side of the island, are the lucky recipients of this dredged sand—eighty thousand cubic feet of it, enough to fill sixteen thousand dump trucks. The

---

† These numbers reflect the early days of COVID-19. Today, as I submit this manuscript, 29,460,286 Americans have tested positive and, tragically, 531,713 Americans have died.

unwanted sand from the channel gushes through a floating pipeline onto our eroding beach, where it is very much appreciated, especially after Hurricane Irma greedily swallowed so much of our shore.

The race, if there is one, is to finish the renourishment project before May 1, the start of turtle season, only a few short weeks away. Or, perhaps, there is a new race—to finish before a possible mandatory shelter-in-place order is issued, where all nonessential businesses will be directed to close. Is renourishing a beach nonessential or essential, considering the turtles and the timing? I have no idea. Ventilators are essential, that much I know.

It's strange, actually, the dredging going on, day and night, juxtaposed against the pandemic these many weeks. I listen to both the news and the hum of the dredge, grateful for the brief moments of quiet when the dredge ceases its raking to take shelter inside the pass, waiting in calmer waters for the wind and bucking waves to tame.

We, too, are sheltering, waiting for the time we no longer need masks to grocery shop or orders to keep a safe distance from one another. We are waiting for the curve to flatten, toilet paper to be readily available, and activities to resume without worry of infection. I am not a hypochondriac but, if I cough more than once, I feel my forehead; my birth date places me squarely in the vulnerable category. If Jim coughs, I irritate him by feeling his forehead as well. Then, sometimes, just in case my palm can't be trusted, I shake down the mercury thermometer, stick it under my tongue (Jim refuses to let me put one under his), and sigh with relief when I see the shimmering silver line hovering just below 98.6.

Last night, I had a COVID-19 nightmare. I was in a packed elevator trying to get out; everyone seemed uncomfortable. Finally, I left the elevator and boarded a bus, trying to get home. Again, everyone crowded into the bus, and there was no bus driver. I climbed into the driver's seat and realized that I had no idea how to drive a bus. None of us knew how to get home without getting too close to other people. My dream is an apt metaphor, I think.

This pandemic is new territory for all of us and, while we know we should not crowd together, no one knows, truthfully, how to navigate this new way of being in the world. Ironically, we are being asked to be alone together.

This evening, Jim and I have taken a break from our vigilance and ventured outside to watch the sun set. Others in our building have emerged, too, some carrying awkward lawn chairs, some sitting on the sea wall, and others perched on benches along the path. We wave and ask, more loudly, *how are you*, all from the safe distance of six feet. I am reminded of small-town America when people ambled to their porches after supper, waving and talking to their neighbors. When the dredging began, social distancing was not part of our lexicon. No one shakes hands or hugs, but we smile, ask about children and grandchildren, and trade stories about how we're keeping connected despite the miles.

I no longer question our decision to cancel our visit to see Mandy and her husband, Jared, in Phoenix, my visit to see three of my sisters in California, and a visit to see friends in Charleston. Most things are canceled or shut down: the park where we play shuffleboard and bocce, our local movie theater, my yoga classes, my meditation group, and our favorite restaurants, although some still offer take-out. I worry about our local businesses that depend upon a profitable tourist season to keep them afloat during the off-season. Can they weather this storm?

For two weeks, now, we have called Candie and Jackie, young new owners of our favorite deli, to order thick chili, creamy tuna salad, and specialty meatballs. I also called our local seafood store and ordered shrimp and crab cakes, which the cashier cheerfully brought to the car to spare us from public exposure to the virus. Even though our home refrigerator is fully stocked, we want Candie, Jackie, and others to stay afloat; we want their refrigerators, and the refrigerators of other businesses, to stay fully stocked as well.

My refrigerator may be full, but my calendar is empty—nothing but open spaces for the first time in years. So blank, I am often not sure what day it is. Despite the warnings and worry streaming across the airwaves and internet, I find a certain deliciousness in this slowing of time. Monday, Tuesday, Wednesday, etc., seem to blend into one another; they seem like nothing more than words, artificially chopping time into nonsensical segments. Today, Wednesday, could just as easily be Tuesday; days seem not to matter in this sheltering place.

Not everyone is sheltering, especially those on the front lines: doctors, nurses, health-care workers, first responders, grocery clerks, Jackie, Candie, and people from all walks of life, many working from home, trying to keep commerce from grinding to a halt. These people are my heroes. In the midst of crisis and disaster, heroes abound—people helping, reaching out, offering their support, and germinating hope.

I am not on the front line, and I humbly realize that my well-being depends on those who are. My efforts to help flatten the curve of COVID-19 boil down to: wash my hands, practice social distancing, and curb unnecessary travel and activities. I can best love my family and friends by staying put, learning to teleconference, sharing recipes that make the most of pantry items, forwarding on bits of humor and meaningful commentaries, explaining how I use a coffee filter inside my bandanna mask, and demonstrating that presence and caring involve more than physical proximity.

Caring is impervious to distance. We, the entire world, are in this together. Perhaps that is why my eyes water when I listen to videos of city-wide claps from balconies and windows in New York City for those on the front lines, or when I hear sequestered Italians singing from their balconies. My friend Mary Ann, who lives in Manhattan, stands on her terrace every night at 7:00 p.m. and rings a bell. She emailed me: *Every night, as the grateful noise, cheers, and energy build, I am in tears.*

Despite the rages of the pandemic, one lone bell or voice, joined by others, sends forth songs of hope and caring that echo around the globe. I can see Mary Ann ringing her bell as tears spill across her smile. Surely, our tears help water the world.

In times of duress or crisis, I would tell my younger self, look about for the heroes, both sung and unsung, for they will surely be there. They will soften the threat of despair. Anyone who attempts to mitigate suffering is a hero. Not all heroes wear uniforms and lab coats; some wear jeans, suits, and other attire. Some make delicious tuna salad, some carry bags to your car, and some simply stand on balconies, clapping and singing hope into the world.

Times of crisis may clear your calendar and blur your days, but they will also awaken you to the importance of love and belonging. Crisis is a time for leaning in, allowing your soul to be excavated; crisis is a time for leaning on, nurturing your network of loved ones; and crisis is a time for leaning out, extending your hand and heart to another.

Today is Thursday. The barge still hums and the sand keeps pumping; so, too, the coronavirus. Our governor just issued a shelter-in-place order, and we have been told someone in our condo building entered the hospital with COVID-19. Hope is my fierce prayer—not only for my neighbor but for our world—no matter how eroded the shore. On the balcony of my soul, I want to throw open my arms and sing about a time, after the waters calm, when we will be renourished. May we be more *widened* and wise; may we recognize our interconnectedness; and may we understand that what happens to one, happens to all.

In the words of Christine Valters Paintner:

> *May we say that love spread more quickly*
> *than a virus ever could.*

—CHRISTINE VALTERS PAINTNER,
ABBEYOFTHEARTS.COM

SLACK TIDE

*A short period when
tidal water is
completely unstressed,
and there is no
movement either way*

The heaviest anguish often precedes a return tide of joy and courage.

—HARRIET BEECHER STOWE[21]

THE RESCUE

I sigh and hang my head. I do not want to see the seagull, but I do. I could ignore it, walk on by without saying a word. I doubt that Mandy, visiting for a few days, has spotted it, hopping on one leg, the other leg hobbled by fishing line, and a fishhook dangling beneath its feathers like an earring. It would be so easy to pretend not to notice. So much easier not to care. But...

"Oh no," I say, touching Mandy's arm and pointing to the gull.

"Oh, Mom," she says, her brown eyes penetrating mine. "What can we do?"

We both know I have rescued several injured birds on this beach, much to my chagrin.

The first time I called the Nature Conservancy, three years ago, I reported that I had spotted a distressed seagull, dragging its broken wing behind it along the sand. "Can you bring it in?" a woman's voice, both kind and imploring, had asked. "We can take it, but we don't have anyone to come get it."

My eyes widened.

"Me? Surely, someone with more experience," I back-pedaled. "I . . . I don't know the first thing . . . or have any idea how to do that. Besides, I don't think it'll let me get close enough."

Truthfully, calling seemed good-Samaritan enough.

"If you can throw a towel over it," she had offered. Her tone indicated I was not her first panicked rescuer. "The towel will calm the gull down so you can pick it up. Then you can bring it to our back door."

What the woman did not seem to understand is that I, too, needed a towel, of sorts, to calm me down. My empathy barely matched my uncertainty; plus, nothing about this potential rescue sounded effortless or convenient.

I sighed, hung up, and paced in front of the window, still not sure if I was up to the task. I continued to watch the befuddled gull drag its limp wing to and fro, looking as pathetic as a lost child dragging her blanket. Every time he fluffed his good wing in an attempt to fly, a piece of me sank deeper into despair.

Finally, I could stand it no longer. I rummaged through our linen closet, pulled out a sun-faded old beach towel, and trekked downstairs. The gull was none too happy to be wound into a towel and plopped into a laundry basket for the duration of our forty-five-minute drive to the back door of the conservancy. Nor was I, fretting whether I was hurting it even more.

But, just as the woman on the phone promised, a technician met me, lifted the gull from the laundry basket, and confidently carried it into a back corridor. "You can call back if you like," she said, over her shoulder. "To see how it's doing."

I did. My seagull survived and was released back on my island.

So, now, today, another seagull's distress has become my own; the fishhook dangles conspicuously beneath its white feathers. Several people momentarily pause to commiserate about its plight. I now know we need a towel, which we don't have. The seagull's legs are tangled together with the fishing line, but it does not appear to be injured. The fishhook has not pierced anything; the reason the gull cannot fly is because the fishing line, binding its legs, is also wrapped around one wing.

"You know, we could probably cut it free," I tell Mandy. "We just need a towel and scissors."

Mandy, our marathon runner, who possesses a heart as big as the Rock of Gibraltar, immediately sprints off toward our condo and calls over her shoulder, "I'll get them."

No reluctance on her part. Her ponytail swishes behind her.

Ten minutes later, she returns carrying a beach towel and scissors. Out of breath, she asks, "What now?"

Indeed. What now?

I open the beach towel and grasp a corner in each hand. I hunch over, as if this posture somehow makes me look smaller and less menacing, and stealthily approach. The seagull is not fooled. It hops farther away. We do this dance several more times before I finally toss the towel and it lands on top of the gull. I am amazed how easily I am able to subdue it.

"You'll have to hold it," I tell Mandy.

Her eyes widen in surprise.

"We'll keep its head covered," I encourage. "But I need

to get to its foot. And we have to be careful of the fish-hook."

I notice my hands shaking slightly. What we have are two novices and a feathered lump in a towel. I take a deep breath and hand the gull to Mandy. We turn, twist, and peel until, finally, a twig-like orange leg pokes out from beneath the folds. I quickly snip off the fishhook and then begin the arduous process of snipping the fishing line away as if I were removing stitches. The gull squirms, and Mandy jumps. "Careful, don't hurt it, Mom," she says.

"He doesn't like it when I tug on the line," I say. "But I can't help it."

The fishing line is tangled in loops around its legs, body, and wing. It never could have freed itself.

"Okay, you can let it go," I finally tell Mandy. She places the towel on the sand and carefully unwraps the gull.

Bewildered, the seagull stands up awkwardly, fluffs its wings, and eyes us. Moments pass. It does not try to fly, probably because so many previous attempts have failed. So Mandy and I wait, smiling at one another until, finally, the gull seems to realize it can walk. And, sure enough, it can also fly.

You will be called upon, more than once, I would tell my younger self, to get involved. Too often we think there is a "they" out there, some amorphous, magnanimous they who will offer a helping hand and take care of the ills of the world for us, a collective, benevolent they who will take charge without involving us. They will look out for us, they will right the wrongs, fight the fight, feed the hungry, and rescue injured birds on the beach. But the truth is, there is no they. There is only "we". We are the they!

It may seem easier not to see or do, but good deeds will not haunt you when you awaken in the middle of the night. Rather, they will uplift you, like a bird taking flight.

Mandy and I continue our walk up the beach. She drapes the towel across her shoulders, I slide the scissors into my pocket, and one more seagull fills the sky.

IKIGAI

The Japanese word *ikigai* (icky-guy), roughly translated, means a person's sense of purpose, one's motivation for climbing out of bed each morning, or, simply, a person's joyful reason for being. Mythologist Joseph Campbell might call it bliss.

This morning, my bliss consists of paddling my kayak toward a small, deserted island, great for beachcombing. My paddle dips left, right, left, right; several droplets of seawater flick onto my forearm and trickle downward toward my wrist. The tide has slackened, making it easier for my paddle to slice through the clouds reflected on the calm surface of the water. The dorsal fin of a dolphin, not far away, dips lazily up and down.

Slack tide marks the tranquil pause of seawater, when the ocean calls time-out from its tidal tug-of-war. I prefer to launch my kayak at slack tide, the quiet, expectant time before the changing of the guard between high and low tide. Slack tide occurs at the end of both ebb and flood tides. Ideally, I paddle out at the end of slack tide and return just as flood tide begins, giving me a little boost back to the kayak launch.

Overhead, a high-pitched, teakettle whistle belongs to an osprey, warning me to steer clear of her nest on the nearby channel marker. She has chicks in the nest, their bandit-mask eyes barely visible above the fortress of sticks. I glide past the marker and angle toward the small beach ahead.

I have paddled far enough to raise a blister on my thumb, which stings as I come ashore. Mimicking the tide, I am pausing for a bit, too, on this deserted beach. I heave the kayak out of the water, banking it above the tide line. Licking the salt off my blister, I plonk my paddle onto the hull and survey this small hectare of sand and mangroves.

The brilliance of the blue sky, combined with the white sand and teal water, reminds me of a postcard my aunt once sent to me from Florida, when I was a child. I could only dream of such a place; my sisters and I lived on the outskirts of a hole-in-the-wall West Texas oil town, with dirt and weeds for a front yard. I fingered my aunt's postcard until the edges yellowed and curled, imagining what it would feel like to visit such a place.

Surrounded now by the sea, all these years later, I know this place to be my ikigai, my bliss. Perhaps, I knew it then even as a child. At this stage of my life, I am happiest in nature. Thoreau had Walden Pond; I am inextricably tied to the sea. Thoreau combed the woods; I comb the beach. Thoreau tried to live deliberately; I try to live mindfully.

As always, when I paddle to this uninhabited island, I comb the beach for shells and bones. Before long, I spy a dazzling, elusive shell, curved perfectly like a wing; its bone-white fluted furrows resemble rows of feathers. I pick it up, brush off the gritty sand, and carry it gingerly, for it chips easily. Aptly named an angel wing, it ranks as one of my top five favorite types of shell. I rarely find an intact specimen on my island.

Interestingly, *gai* in the word ikigai comes from the word *kai,* meaning shell in Japanese; it refers to a period when shells were deemed valuable.[22] I have only one question. When were shells not valuable?

However, my motivation for getting up this morning was not to find shells, but to find joy. The Dalai Lama believes that finding happiness is the main purpose of life,[23] a deep-rooted happiness based on joy. I wholeheartedly agree. I have the luxury, at this stage of my life, to excavate joy from my days, no matter the direction they take. Rarely is a day devoid of at least one act of kindness, one frame of beauty, or thirty thousand breaths of life. Joyful moments abound, scattered like seashells alongside the sea.

There were times, in early motherhood, when I thought *doing* was far more valuable than *being*. If I had a blank hour or day on the calendar and someone asked me if I could do something—meet for lunch, attend a meeting, be room mom, write a newsletter, host a gathering—I felt compelled to say yes because I didn't have a conflicting time commitment. I said yes, over and over again, until one day I woke so completely depleted that I almost ended up in the hospital with upper respiratory distress.

My overpacked calendar had sapped not only my energy but my joy. It occurred to me that I did not have to say yes—even if my calendar were empty. I began to check in with my internal calendar and came to understand that the white spaces on my calendar were actually appointments with well-being. I began to allot time and space to discover joy and renourish my spirit.

This is what slack tide affords.

Today, my ikigai, my bliss, is kayaking to a solitary beach, communing with nature, finding an angel wing, and writing about it. I do not know if this will add more years to my life, but I do know it adds bliss to all the years of life I have left.

Allot fallow time for being, I would tell my younger self. Create space in your life to ponder and follow your bliss. Make a date with well-being and ask yourself: If I could have any life I wanted, what life would I choose? What do I like to do when I don't have to do anything? What are my little joys?

The tides and currents of time will take you to new shores, but you don't need an outside compass to find your way. Rely on your internal compass, the one that makes your heart skip a beat when you discover a new skill or idea; the one that may lead you off a well-traveled path toward the wilds of who you are and what you are capable of doing; the one that makes your heart yearn to paddle in calm waters, among dolphins, toward an uninhabited island, where the wing of an angel awaits your arrival.

Slack tide has given way to the incoming tide. Inhaling the sky's blueness, I paddle the kayak back toward the inhabited world. My angel wing and I glide silently across the calm surface. Water droplets fall from my paddle and splash onto my arms. The sprinkling of cool water feels like a blessing.

BOCCE BABES

The early-morning beach plow has left claw prints on the sand. The eight of us look for a suitable spot, someplace where the sand packs closer together. We share unspoken chores; two women drop six orange cones marking off the court, as close to ten feet by forty-eight feet as the eye can tell.

"I think that cone needs to go a little to the left," someone says. "How about that one?" another asks, pointing to the right. Every woman's eyes measure the distance a little differently. "I think that's good," our matriarch, Joan, says, so named because she reached out and started this group, which has been a gift to each of us.

Another woman pulls out two sets of movable beads we use to keep score, twelve beads to a string. We play by our own rules. I hold a bag for each woman to reach in and draw a piece of laminated paper with either the word *red* or *green*, which not only represents the color of our wooden bocce balls, four red and four green, but also determines our teams.

Today, I'm a member of the Green Team. I loft my two-pound green ball toward a smaller white target ball, called a jack or pallino. (Actually, our pallino isn't white anymore; we glammed it up by gluing on brightly colored paper to make it more visible in the sand.) I lean my body left, as if to help guide my ball's trajectory.

"Great shot," several ladies cheer when it snuggles against the festive pallino. It feels good to land a decent shot; I am mediocre at best.

My success, however, may be short-lived. One of the better players, on the last throw, fires her red ball and hits mine away. It's hard to tell which of our balls is closer. Dutifully, someone retrieves our state-of-the-art measuring device, a tin can with a knotted string in the center, a rather ingenious invention, actually, which of course someone decorated with pretty contact paper.

That's what I love about these ladies: they have personality. We wear matching T-shirts that say Bocce Babes; a red bocce ball replaces the letter *o* in Bocce and a voluptuous set of red lips underscores the word *Babes*. Every Monday in-season, from January through April, eight of us meet on the beach at nine thirty to play bocce. We are in our sixth season.

After some back-and-forth discussion about my green ball and the red one, and a lot of measuring, because only centimeters separate the two, it is determined that the red ball is closer. Drat. The red team advances a bead closer to twelve.

Before the game ends, I notice a police car idling toward us, routinely patrolling the beach and enforcing beach rules, like no pets or glass containers. The officer, in short sleeves, rests his elbow casually atop his open window as he approaches, evidently amused by this over-fifty Bocce Babes game. He nods and raises his fingers.

I risk a joke.

"The reason I called you," I yell to him, "is because there has been some disagreement about a ball I threw."

Stunned silence. He breaks into a wide grin. Everyone laughs. Our laughter feels as warm and welcoming as the sunlight hugging my shoulders. What impresses me most about this group of women is not our prowess, not our great and not-so-great shots, not winning or losing. No, what impresses me most is our camaraderie, the way we have bonded over the years, the way we went from strangers to acquaintances to friends.

Only in recent years have I come to realize the vital role women's groups have played in fostering my growth and unfolding. My sisters were my first circle of women; we leaned mightily on one another while trying to navigate our tumultuous childhood. Later, I continued to be drawn to various circles—exploring dreams, meditation, and spirituality—but I didn't fully recognize the significance of those gatherings back then.

In hindsight, I see that those heterogeneous groups introduced me to people, ideas, and personalities that I might never have sought out on my own. The biggest lesson I have learned is that unconditional positive regard hinges more on *getting to know* than on being homogenous. A group, like my bocce group, fosters community and belonging. We women have undergone an alchemical process of sorts, transmuting lead into gold. A decade ago we were strangers. Today, we're more like sisters.

Gather a group of women around you, I would encourage my younger self. Adjust your boundaries to focus on what you have in common rather than your differences. Most everyone, no matter their politics, no matter their faith, no matter the color of their team, no matter their heritage, wants to feel happy, safe, loved, valued, and included. People are more alike than different. Celebrate your common ground; allow laughter and compassion to transmute lead into gold; foster a sense of belonging and camaraderie. And, should a dispute ever arise, allow love to measure the distance between you.

After two games, it's time to pack up. One to one. My favorite score. We pick up the orange cones, load our cart, and meander back toward the condo, sharing bits of news. Someone's daughter is expecting a baby, another has to fly north for a christening, and yet another is worried about her aging father.

I turn and look back at our court, which is covered in mingling footprints—just like the intertwining of our lives.

HOMECOMING

Ore than my tires hum as I cross our island bridge. No matter that this may be my ten-thousandth crossing. At the uppermost arc of the bridge, the unmistakable feeling of homecoming swirls in my chest as the island bursts into view. I never tire of this salt-water paradise, throwing open its arms of welcome.

Short distances to the left, three small mangrove islands, the ABCs, stand at attention in the open expanse of water. Combined, these three islands comprise a one-hundred-year-old rookery, a rookery that welcomes thousands of birds every year. Designated as a critical wildlife area, a three-hundred-foot buffer zone protects the rookery. No boats or people are allowed closer than the distance of a football field.

Unfortunately, there is no protective buffer zone for the shorebirds that sometimes congregate on our island's white sandy beach. Constantly flushing birds into flight exhausts them and causes them to weaken, leaving them without the necessary energy to survive and forage for food. I learned this firsthand after I rescued a lethargic, disoriented seagull. After I dropped the gull off at the conservancy and called some days later to check on it, I was told the gull needed only food and rest to recover. They told me that the competition for resources had weakened him.

I wish I could relay that seagull's plight to beach walkers and children, who innocently delight in flushing shorebirds into flight, unaware that their chasing game harms the shorebirds; it might even cause some to die. If people knew this, I'm sure more care would be taken. I didn't know flushing birds harmed them when Mandy was a child. I even have pictures of her running into flocks, the birds lifting in unison. What I lacked back then, though, was awareness, not compassion. Now that I am aware, I take more care to walk around a flock of birds on my beach walks, instead of plowing straight through the middle of them.

So, for people unaware, like I was, I am grateful that the ABCs are off-limits. The birds need a safe sanctuary. Sometimes as many as ten thousand shorebirds—herons, anhingas, brown pelicans, cormorants, and dozens of other species—roost and nest on the ABCs, as if privy to the three-hundred-foot mandate that keeps them from being disturbed. Sometimes, at sunset, Jim and I watch different flocks of birds from our balcony, some just skimming the water's surface, heading home for the night to roost. They most always fly south and then veer east at the pass, in the direction of the ABCs.

Birds inhabit the ABCs in daylight as well, some nesting and raising chicks. This afternoon, from my vantage point at the top of the bridge, I spot dozens of snowy egrets perched majestically like tree ornaments; their feathery crowns and breast plumes contrast against the green of the mangroves. Above them, long-tailed frigates pepper the sky, hanging like kites, riding on the wind.

On the other side of the bridge, as familiar to me as the ABCs, lies an ever-changing sandbar that keeps boaters guessing; for years it has shape-shifted according to the whims of the currents and storms. Docks edge the water, poised with boats with names like *At the Office*, *No Worries*, and *Reel Therapy*. Beyond the docks sits Rose Marina, home to our dinner-cruise ship, eco-tours, and a high-speed ferry that connects us to Key West (well worth the visit to see Hemingway's home and the descendants of his six-toed cats).

Beyond Rose Marina, near the northeast corner of the island, stands our favorite casual eatery, serving up the best fried shrimp, fresh from the Gulf. Beyond the condos and hotels, in the distant blue haze ahead of me, lies a gleaming jewel, the Gulf of Mexico.

For me, all of these sights equate to home, that place that feels like a warm embrace.

Whenever I return after dark and see the bridge lamps arching into the night, I remember my grandma and grandpa's glowing, farm-house porch light, welcoming us to a refuge of calm, free from the chaos of our transient life and Mama's discontent. I think it fair to say that Mama lacked awareness back then; she did not lack compassion. She did not realize how her flushings—her insistence that we pick up and leave, sometimes hurriedly stuffing our clothing into a box or paper bag *to get the hell out of there*—taxed the well-being of my sisters and me.

Grandma and Grandpa's farm turned out to be our

rookery, a buffer zone of fields, moss-laden oaks, and a tin-roofed farmhouse. The tin roof glinted with sunlight when the sky shone blue and pinged with rain when the clouds overflowed. When our family neared my grand-parents' farm at the end of our hours-long journey to visit them, I narrowed my eyes, searching for the first glimpse of that single porch-light bulb, peeking through the trees. As we crossed the trickling branch, which was sometimes a washed-out gully, I felt an unmistakable swirl in my chest when my eyes locked on the porch bulb's steadfast glare. Grandpa would be up and waiting, no matter how late our arrival. His hug felt safe, warm, and inviting, the longed-for feeling of homecoming.

That same feeling of homecoming swirls in my chest when I cross the bridge onto our island. Like the birds, returning to roost in their trees, we all need a safe place to alight, a place as welcoming and life-giving as a grandpa's hug.

Don't underestimate the importance of homecoming, I would tell my younger self. Our soul needs a place to roost, a place to soar on the currents of time, a protected place, buffered from the outside world.

Don't entrust your well-being to those who are unconscious or unaware. Erect a buffer zone around that which is precious.

Continue to learn, grow, and expand in order to cultivate more awareness. If you discover you have unknowingly taxed another, vow to do better going forward, make amends, and learn from your mistake. It does no good to scold yourself for what you do not know. But the same holds true for those who unknowingly tax you. This generosity of spirit recognizes the compassionate heart, much like that of an innocent child flushing birds.

Someday, when you reach my age, you may see glimmers of a different light peeking through the trees, and a different bridge welcoming you home. Nothing to fear—your soul knows the way. Perhaps Grandpa will be waiting up for you with the porch light blazing, ready to enfold you in a welcome-home hug.

I continue over the bridge, past our modest, welcome-to-our-island sign. The speed limit drops to thirty miles per hour. More than my car slows down; the pace softens here. The time is near nine—we call it *island midnight*. The sidewalks clear, and lights appear in windows like stars in the sky.

I turn down our street. Date palms replace the moss-draped oaks of my grandpa's farm, but I see the same familiar light—the warm glow of home.

LEGACY

Standing on the marina dock with my friend Pam, I take note of what I call *cloud moon*, the waning crescent moon that, in daylight, looks like a pale wisp in the blue eye of sky. I am confident today will be a lucky day for us. If not, I might quietly sing, "Dolphins, come unto us," a song I taught Mandy years ago.

The song is an adaptation of a chant I learned from Brooke Medicine Eagle, a tribal wise woman who wrote *Buffalo Woman Comes Singing.* What I most admire about Brooke and her lineage is her promotion of a heart-centered, ecologically sound belief in healing *Mother Earth and all our relations.* This is why I love the excursion we're about to take; it fosters a deep sense of caring for the earth and her creatures—especially dolphins, noted for their seemingly altruistic behavior.

"Let's head for the back of the boat," I suggest to Pam as we prepare to board the forty-seven-foot catamaran. "That's the best place to see them jump."

It tickles me to introduce Pam to this experience. We

both love the island and enjoy being on the water, which is why it surprised me to learn that Pam has never taken this tour.

"You're in for a treat," I told her when she first agreed to come.

Pam shares some of my adventuresome nature; we have also kayaked and ridden bikes together. I admire Pam's easy laugh, tender heart, and most especially her tenacity. Even though she lost her husband, Lynn, six years ago, she soldiers on. Lynn has missed his daughters' weddings and the births of his grandchildren, although Pam would tell you he was there in spirit. This I do not dispute.

Visor in hand, Pam grabs the railing and steps onto the boat, her flip-flops flicking against her heels. The space smells of the zinc oxide a mother slathers onto her young son.

"Hello again," Captain Mike says when he sees me. I see my reflection in his blue-lensed sunglasses. I flash him a wide grin, happy to be recognized, especially since I consider myself to be a frequent flyer of sorts.

"I've brought a friend today," I say, nudging Pam. "She's never been."

Captain Mike strums the steering wheel, nods, and smiles at Pam. "Welcome. Glad to have you aboard," he says.

Pam may well be my hundredth guest on the *Dolphin Explorer*, a dolphin study and eco-tour outfit. It's the only ongoing study of wild dolphins in southwest Florida that names, codes, and catalogs over one hundred coastal bottlenose dolphins. The program tracks travel range, movement, social patterns, behavior, and the genealogy of our local dolphins.

When anyone visits the island or asks what my favorite thing to do is, I encourage them to take this tour. Mandy, my dolphin-singing partner and an environmental lawyer and sustainability expert, shares my enthusiasm. She gives me *Dolphin Explorer* gift certificates for my birthday and Mother's Day, which I insist she help me use.

Bob and Kent, the two naturalists who split the tours, have begun to recognize me, just as I have come to know what they will say before they say it:

- Think of the boat as a clock: the bow is twelve o'clock. When you see a dolphin, instead of yelling "over there," say, "dolphin at three o'clock" or "dolphin at nine o'clock."
- See that bird's nest on the channel marker? That's an osprey nest.
- The dolphins in this area generally give birth sometime between September and November.
- Mangroves are the only tree species that can grow in salt water.

Sometimes I envy Bob and Kent's job. I imagine myself on the water, wind ruffling my hair, as my eyes seek a dorsal fin breaking the water or as I point out a mangrove forest or a dozen other wonders in our ten-thousand-island area.

As it happens, Pam and I are too late to secure a seat in the stern. Two other groups, either knowingly or accidentally, have placed themselves in the perfect location should any dolphins decide to leap and frolic in the boat's wake during the tour. We take our seats starboard side, more toward the middle of the boat.

I feel a bit uneasy. *What if we don't see any dolphins?* I want Pam's experience to live up to my billing.

Captain Mike starts to motor out of the marina, and anticipation builds. *Who doesn't love dolphins?* I wonder. Then a shiver goes through me. I know for a fact that some human hearts, traversing these waters, find no pleasure or joy in these mammals.

"Have you heard about the recent dolphin killings?" I ask Pam.

She shakes her head no, her expression both pained and surprised.

I read about it days earlier. The news weighs on me like an anchor. Captain Mike nods that he knows about it, too. A dolphin washed up with a bullet hole in its head; then, three days later, another dolphin washed up, fatally shot or speared; months before that, still another. Not all harmed dolphins wash up on the beach; the numbers might be higher.

People's outrage heartens me. The National Oceanic and Atmospheric Administration announced a $20,000 reward for anyone with information on the deaths. Several agency partners have increased the reward to $54,000.[24] Thus far, no one has come forward.

Most Florida residents know that harassing, hunting, or killing wild dolphins is against the law. Even feeding them is against the law; it causes dolphins to associate people with food, which can put them in harmful situations. Violations can be steep—punishable with fines up to $100,000 and a year in jail.

Bob teeters as the bow crests over a wave. He widens his stance to stabilize himself and officially begins the tour. Predictably, he tells us to think of the boat as a clock.

My problem with the clock analogy is that my mind pictures twelve o'clock directly in front of me, no matter if I'm facing the stern or the bow. I find myself shouting, "Dolphin at three, no, nine," and then saying exactly what Bob has told us not to say, "Dolphin, over there," which offers Captain Mike no idea of which way to turn the boat.

Bob holds up large blue binders, filled with dozens of photographs. "Today, you're going to help us identify the dolphins we see, using these catalogs," he tells us, passing out the binders.

Pam wrangles one of the blue binders onto her lap and thumbs through dozens of photographs that picture only one thing: a close-up of a dorsal fin. Typed beneath each unique fin is the name of a particular dolphin. Every dolphin's dorsal fin is as distinctive as a human fingerprint. Each has its own thickness, height, shape, and markings. From birth, dolphins' fins are marked by playful or instructional nips from other dolphins, entanglements with fishing lines, damage from boat propellers, or other environmental conditions. No two fins bear the same markings.

"Nine o'clock," someone yells.

Captain Mike eases the throttle and turns the boat eastward. Then Pam and I see it—a large dorsal fin lazily breaking the water. Bob focuses his telephoto lens and begins clicking. Captain Mike slows the boat so we can observe. We hear a distinct *phew* of air expelled from the dolphin's blowhole as it rises and dips again.

After some minutes, Bob nods to Mike, indicating he got a good shot of the dorsal fin for their records. Continuing the tour, Captain Mike slowly increases our speed, and the dolphin begins to follow our boat. I smile. I know exactly what happens next.

Sure enough, the grinning dolphin explodes out of the water behind our boat. People rush toward the back, their cell phones poised. Collective squeals of delight and laughter drown out the sound of the motor as the dolphin continues to leap, sometimes as much as six feet into the air. Before each leap, I know to look for it, streaming just beneath the surface of the water, as though it's swimming through a waterfall. "Look, there," I say pointing to its streamlined body picking up more and more speed until, like a torpedo, it blasts through the wake and into the air. More squeals and delight.

I turn to Pam, who is holding aloft her cell. "Did you get it?"

She smiles and nods. "On video."

A twenty-something, tan woman watches the video over Pam's shoulder. "If I give you my email, will you email it to me?"

"Sure," Pam says.

No doubt Pam's daughters and grandchildren will love the video, too. "It may go viral," I tease.

As we cruise farther, we see more dolphins. Bob passes around three photographs of dorsal fins he has taken thus far. By matching the fins to the photographs in the blue catalog, we can identify the dolphins. The inner curve of the first dorsal fin resembles the jagged blade of a sawtooth pruner. We discover the fin belongs to our first jumping dolphin, named C.U. Jimmie, a male dolphin who often hangs out by himself.

The second dorsal fin resembles the sloping shape of the Matterhorn. Looking through the book, we discover this dorsal fin belongs to Hatchet and, consequently, we know the other dolphin beside Hatchet must be Capri, because these two boys can always be found together. They have created a male-pair bond alliance, second only to the bonding of a mother and calf. I have seen Capri and Hatchet together most every trip; they like to feed against the seawall near the mouth of the Gulf. We also see Halfway, identified by one notch in the center of her fin. Halfway is the most prolific mother of the study; she has given birth every three years for the past eighteen years.

If a new, unnamed baby is spotted on tour, the passengers get to name it. I have never been lucky enough to see this. However, since most of the births occur between September and November, I try to schedule at least one fall trip. My name of choice would be Jewel, short for Jewel of the Sea.

I look about at the excited, wide-eyed visitors. This dolphin study not only tracks dolphins, it fosters a sense of care for them. Far from wanting to harm dolphins, the children and adults on board have forged a genuine connection with them. As a memento, Bob passes out a photograph of C.U. Jimmie, smiling, jumping the wake, and winnowing his way into our hearts.

We are the stewards of Mother Earth and all her relations, I would tell my younger self. What an incredible home upon which we live. Share your love of the natural world with friends and family—especially your daughter. Teach her to care about all of it: the land, the trees, and the oceans. Be her mentor and model. In addition to loving her, let your legacy be your love for nature. Take her outside and point up to the sky; sit under a tree; dance in the rain; sing to the dolphins; wade in the sea.

Respect, kindness, and concern are the antidotes of cruelty; they keep the heart pliable and, yes, more vulnerable. Her heart may get nicked and scarred, making it uniquely her own, but the hardened heart knows not the joy of reveling, honoring, or belonging. Your reward will be great. Trust me. She will grow up to defend this planet you so dearly love. She will shed a tear when she witnesses cruelty. But, greatest of all, she will gift you with adventures and stand beside the future you, with graying temples, softly singing a dolphin song into your ear.

Captain Mike steers the boat back into the marina, and Bob holds out his rough hand to steady us as we climb from the boat. Several children clutch the dolphin activity worksheet Bob handed out earlier. Bob's toothy smile signals his approval as he tells the children they are now junior members of the Explorer's survey team. One girl reminds me of a young Mandy; she looks especially pleased—a new environmentalist in the making.

And so it goes.

The *Dolphin Explorer*'s legacy is forging a bond with the natural world. My legacy is passing on the baton of loving the earth and sharing my dolphin-watching certificates. Mandy's legacy is her concern for the environment and gifting me with dolphin-watching certificates. Halfway's legacy is giving us more dolphins. Pam's legacy is forging a strong family in Lynn's absence and probably planning a dolphin tour for her grandchildren.

Dolphins, come unto us. . . .

TIME-OUT

I retrieve a painted five-by-seven-inch wooden sign from the pantry shelf and clack it against the kitchen counter. Rimmed in sun yellow, the sign depicts the seashore, complete with gulls, a bucket of shells, and the words *Gone Shelling* written in script across the bottom.

I purchased the sign to avoid writing the same note over and over. Whenever Jim wakes to find the sign displayed on the kitchen counter, sometimes beside a plate of scrambled eggs and crisp bacon, he knows not to worry about where I am or how long I'll be gone. The sign is my way of saying time-out, I am climbing into a Narnian wardrobe, of sorts, where time bends and disappears. I am entering a doorway outside time, on a shore bejeweled with shells, and it may be a while before I find my way back.

I revel in these time-outs. When I get lost in a good book, or string words together in a paragraph, or succumb to the siren's call of a jigsaw puzzle, I lose track of time. Suddenly, I *wake up* and discover time moved on without me. This also happens when I tumble into deep conversations, pore over old photographs, and, quite frequently, when I comb the beach looking for seashells.

Combing the beach tops my list this morning.

Ironically, I owe my fondness for shelling to a one-min-ute encounter with a stranger, many years ago. It happened on vacation, early one Thanksgiving morning. I woke early to walk the beach, oblivious to the seashells scattered about me, no doubt trying to mentally figure out which fork to follow on the meandering path of life. I did, however, notice a woman walking toward me; wisps of gray tendrils danced about her face as she swayed a bucket to and fro. She looked to be a perfect grandmother to some lucky child.

When her eyes met mine, I smiled.

She surprised me by reaching into her bucket and with-drawing something. "Happy Thanksgiving," she said, offer-ing me a shell.

"Happy . . . Thanksgiving," I stammered. I cupped my hand to receive her offering.

"It's a turkey wing," she explained, placing it lightly in my palm. "Doesn't it look like the real thing?"

I turned the handsome shell over in my hand. Its shape resembled an outstretched wing, patterned in brown and white stripes that looked remarkably like the wing of a wild turkey. Amazed at the likeness and the timing of Thanks-giving Day, I readily agreed. "It really does look like a wing," I said. "Thank you so much."

She nodded and smiled, pleased that I was pleased.

"Happy Thanksgiving," I said again as she continued on.

I examined the shell more closely; its edges showed the wear of tumbling in the surf. How was it that I had never paid much attention to the different shells at my feet? Every shell was a stranger to me. Suddenly, I wanted to know the names of them all.

I bought several shelling books, a bucket and trowel, and baby oil to rub on the seashells after I washed and dried them. I learned shelling etiquette: do not collect live shells, keep a respectful distance from others who are shelling, avoid walking on and crushing shells on the shell line where others are shelling, and, if possible, return stranded shells and sea critters back to the water—which I plan to do this very minute.

I see a stranded sea critter. I stop, drop my sandals, and pick up a nine-armed sea star, marooned by the tide. The tube feet on the starfish's underside feel bristly against my fingers as they move in an undulating fashion. I wade into the cool salt water and toss the sea star gently, like a Frisbee, and it splashes into the rolling surf. Oddly, returning it to its watery home feels consequential in an inconsequential way.

Beauty and peace blanket the morning. Hundreds of seashells lie scattered along the shoreline. Just above the shoreline, lithe, limber bodies in a beach yoga class pose in warrior, downward dog, and cobra. As the students bow to their colorful yoga mats, spread upon the sand like magic carpets, I bow to the shore.

Over and over, I bend and bow. My mind rests only here, in the morning, listening to the waves, and feeling the coolness of sand beneath my feet. I pick up a moon shell with its hieroglyphic markings curved along its circumference. Next to it, I spot a spiny jewel box; its frilly, hollow spines resemble carved ivory.

I think it fair to say I know the common name of the majority of shells on our island: cat's paws, lady slippers, shark eyes, junonias, baby ears, top shells, and dozens more. Our island's cornucopia of shells delights most collectors. On rare occasions, I have found several giant, spiraling whelks; their size and inner chambers, dark and mysterious, enamor me.

Conchologists study shells. I am, perhaps, an amateur conchologist, continually interested in learning more about the bivalves and univalves that I collect. Bivalves, like scallops, have two shells that open and close; univalves, like whelks and conchs, have only one shell. The gastropod inside a univalve has a hard, flat operculum (resembling the composition of an animal horn) that closes like a door to protect the shell's interior. My collection includes several opercula as well as several parchment-like egg casings of whelks.

However, no univalve or bivalve need fear me; I am not a predator. I never collect live shells, no matter how beautiful. Harvesting live shells is illegal in our county, and, in counties where it is legal, one needs a Florida recreational saltwater fishing license, even if harvesting from the beach.[25]

My harvest of empty, legal shells clacks in my bag. I look to the sun to estimate the time. How long ago did I plop the Gone Shelling sign onto the kitchen counter? An hour ago? Maybe an hour and a half? It matters little.

Every morning, for thousands of years, the sea has stroked this shore. And every morning, for thousands of years to come, the sea will continue to stroke this shore. I find solace in this; I find strength to be optimistic about the world's future; I find fortitude to love my brother and sister across the aisle; I find joy, despite life's tribulations.

Time-outs are good for the soul.

I turn for home, my bag swinging to and fro.

Time-outs are good for the soul, I would tell my younger self. Take the time to step outside time. Solace, strength, and joy are yours for the taking. Lose yourself in a Narnian wardrobe; take a time-out from worry, fear, and angst. Don't be blind to the everyday beauty and magic scattered so generously all about you. Be curious; follow the curve of a seashell into wonder. Find a doorway to the eternal present.

Complete strangers may touch your life in profound ways. Be open to receive the gifts of such encounters, and be mindful that you, too, might be an unnamed stranger to someone else on their journey. If the simple act of offering a shell can ripple outward, years afterward, imagine the impact of a smile, a gesture, or a kind word. You may never know how a kindness impacts another, but you can be sure it leaves its footprint on you—even something as inconsequential as tossing a sea star into the sea. Don't be careless with these encounters, for actions, both good and bad, lap against the shores of time, long after we are gone.

And look over there. See that older woman bowing to the shore, collecting seashells? Send her a blessing. You may be her someday.

I return from my time-out; the smell of bacon still lingers in the kitchen. Jim has yet to rise. I replace the Gone Shelling sign on the pantry shelf. The clock says I have been gone for almost an hour and half, but I cannot be sure.

It's impossible to measure Narnian time with hour hands.

WHITE HORSES

I have no way of knowing, as I look out to sea, that I will be incapacitated by the end of the day.

As it is, a light breeze flutters the collar of my cotton shirt, tickling my neck. From my perch on the lanai, I peruse the Gulf, looking for white horses. Not white horses that gallop across open fields, or the prancing white Lipizzaner stallions I once admired from my arena seat in Vienna, or, sadly, even a winged white horse I named Samson, who often lifted me aloft in my dreams. Samson transported me to the inner recesses of my psyche and helped me discover my own autonomy. Even today, I am nostalgic for Samson's unbridled, broad back, my fingers gripping his coarse mane, and the winds of my imagination blowing through my hair.

This morning, however, I am searching for a different kind of white horse, the white horses mentioned in the two-hundred-year-old Beaufort Wind Scale, still used by the National Weather Service.[26] The scale's originator, Admiral Beaufort, refers to whitecaps as white horses, presumably because waves take on the look of a horse's mane flowing across the waters, and waves sound like hooves when they thunder onto shore. No wonder the Greeks credited Poseidon, their god of the sea, with creating the first horse.

Jim and I have adopted the white-horse nomenclature. We use it to help us determine wind speed. We plan to ride bikes this morning and don't like to ride when it is too windy. Riding with the wind is easy, breezy; I love the feeling of a gentle breeze blowing across my face. But riding against a brisk wind saps my strength and causes my quadriceps to cramp. Jim's racer bike outnumbers the gears on my cruiser by eighteen. Plus, I wear a broad brim attached to my bike helmet to protect me from the sun; it's effective, but I look like Sally Field wearing her cornet headdress in *The Flying Nun*. Even on the calmest days, my brim lifts as I ride.

Based on Beaufort's visual descriptions, I guess us to be four on his scale of one to twelve, four being a moderate breeze of thirteen to eighteen miles per hour: "Small waves, becoming larger; fairly frequent white horses. Raises dust and loose paper; small branches are moved."[27] At four, the water horses do not stampede the shore; rather, they canter and dance like Lipizzaner stallions, stirring up the waters but posing no real threat.

Our bike ride is on.

An hour later, after airing up our tires, pedaling to Doreen's Cup of Joe for breakfast, and taking the last bite of my create-your-own-omelet, I rise to freshen up before riding to the park. I love our park; it's my favorite place to ride and picnic. It reminds me of small-town America, where locals gather to play bocce and shuffleboard and youngsters come to play on the fields, playground, and basketball courts. Jim and I usually park our bikes and play several games of shuffleboard before returning home.

As I stand up from the table, my body moves forward, but my left foot has fallen asleep and feels like a wooden log; it has wedged behind the table trestle. The next few seconds unfold in slow motion. I tug my unresponsive foot, try to keep my balance, and call to mind the balancing postures of tai chi, but to no avail—my foot remains stuck. I topple, graceless as a felled tree, in front of two wide-eyed patrons finishing their breakfast.

When Jim turns to see me lying on the restaurant floor, I say, "I heard a loud pop. I think my ankle may be broken."

Jim helps me hobble to my seat, my ankle already throbbing. Great, I think. We have ridden our bikes, and I won't be able to ride home. I notice that I'm feeling light-headed, but, thankfully, because everything happened in slow motion, I know I didn't hit my head. The astonished couple, at the table for two, also confirmed this. Feeling even woozier, I bend down to place my head between my knees, and I wake to find Jim standing over me.

I wake a second time to see other people gathered around me, trying to keep me in my chair. I wake a third time to see the face of a police officer, who is saying the ambulance is on its way. Worry etches Jim's face as he stands over me saying, "Oh, Terry."

I wake a fourth and final time on the gurney being loaded into the ambulance.

"How are you feeling?" the EMT asks me.

"Foolish," I answer.

"Besides foolish," he says kindly.

"Just light-headed," I say as I'm hooked up to a heart

monitor by one EMT while the other one finds a vein in the bend of my elbow to insert a port for fluids. "This is going to sting a little," he tells me.

"Low blood pressure," the other EMT tells his partner.

Jim is not with me; he was told he would have to follow. He has no car, only our two bikes and my headdress bike helmet.

I feel like I'm in a dream, riding bareback on Samson to some internal landscape, but soon realize I'm jostling on a gurney, being transported over the island bridge to the nearest hospital. I don't lose consciousness again, but my mind floats. I am not invincible. I can lose my balance no matter how many years I practice tai chi. I am no longer climbing the hill of life, with no view of the finish line. I can see the finish line now; it is much closer than the start line.

Mandy cannot imagine this world without me in it. I don't want to let her down. Every day, to help manifest my intention to live a long, happy life, I get dressed while looking at that congratulatory one-hundred-year birthday card I bought for myself and taped to the inside of my closet door. May I live to actually celebrate my one hundredth birthday with a sixty-eight-year-old Mandy by my side. But I am mortal. I realize this. I am a white horse, amid countless other white horses, rising and cresting on this great sea of life.

This I know, I would tell my younger self. The wave is mortal, but the water from which the wave rises continues on. We are spiritual beings having a human experience. Like waves, our bodies rise and crest, but our essence returns to spirit. Cherish this human experience with every fiber of your being, I would encourage, but, also, allow yourself opportunities to ride to the center of your being, to connect to that essence within you that is as eternal as the sea, that place from which we spring and return. Find your autonomy and, paradoxically, your connection to all that is.

I lie in a bed, curtained off in the emergency room. X-rays show that my ankle is not broken—just a severe sprain. The wavy lines on the EKG indicate no heart attack, and a stroke has been ruled out. Jim peeks through the curtain; the restaurant owner drove him and our two bikes home so Jim could get the car. He's relieved to find me sitting up and finishing the bag of intravenous fluids. Evidently, pain and shock caused my blood pressure to dip so low that I couldn't maintain consciousness.

On our drive home, we call Mandy and Jared and assure them all is well. I learn that Jared had already checked out flight schedules, just in case. Jim squeezes my hand hard. He's already figuring out how to get crutches. I take in the sight of him, this man who has stood by my side for more than fifty years. Like two draft horses, we are stronger together than either one of us alone.

My heart hums with the tires as we cross the bridge. I feel such gratitude—for life, for family, for the restaurant owner who drove Jim home, and for the EMTs who treated me so kindly. Taking in the sunny view from the top of the bridge, I see a few prancing white horses in the sparkling waters below. I may be temporarily hobbled, but soon my mane will be flowing in the gentle breezes of an early-morning bike ride.

NAMING STARS

It's 3:00 a.m. I often wake in the middle of the night, and while this interruption used to annoy me, I since have made peace with this early-morning hour that seeks my companionship. Some clairvoyants suggest a deceased loved one may be trying to connect with us before the busyness of day sets in—an intriguing thought, and a comforting one, too. Perhaps the veils between worlds thin at this hour. Sometimes, just in case, I give a nod to my ancestors. I whisper hello and think of my sister Nancy, or my mom, or my colorful aunt Betty, or my grandparents.

Then I usually read, work a puzzle, or listen to an audiobook. Or, on nights like tonight, I make my way outside to commune with the stars and listen to the sea whispering to the shore. Hugging my shawl about my shoulders, I settle into a lounge chair and tuck my knees beneath my chin. The sea shushes like a mother rocking her child to sleep.

At this hour of night, my eyes have had time to adapt to the darkness, making the stars seem brighter. Tonight's sky reminds me of my mother's blue-black hair studded with her rhinestone bobby pins, her thick, voluminous hair, aglitter with light. The brightest rhinestoned night I ever beheld occurred on safari in Africa.

I rarely slept on that African safari, so enamored was I with the night sky and falling stars. The sky, blanketed with twinkling lights, looked more white than black; I held up my thumb toward the heavens and could barely find a thumb width of darkness between the stars. It was the loveliest look at infinity I have ever seen. Stars shine continuously; they don't go anywhere during the day, or when it storms, or when ambient light dims their visibility. They forever shine, seen or unseen.

My eyes search, now, for the glimmering Seven Sisters; I am partial to these stars because, on my star chart, they represent my six sisters and me. I pinpoint their hazy shimmer. Even though my sister Nancy no longer exists on earth, she dances, still, with the Seven Sisters above, visible from almost anywhere on the globe, even Africa. Also called the Pleiades, the Seven Sisters make up the nearest star cluster to Earth, a mere four hundred light-years away. I reason that I am looking at light that began its journey to Earth when our great-great-great-great-great-great-great-great-great-great-great-great-grandmother was born.

The three stars of Orion's belt shine to the southwest of the Seven Sisters. For thirty-eight years, Jim, Mandy, and I have pointed to those three stars, saying, "There's our family." After Mandy married, we designated a fourth star to represent her husband, Jared. He has been added to our constellation.

And then there is Delphinus, a small constellation said to be placed in the heavens by Poseidon, who declared the dolphin sacred and placed its image among the stars. Over a decade ago, my friend Sue and I bought a star in Delphinus.

Well, not exactly.

We bought the right to unofficially name a star, which synchronistically happened to be in the constellation Delphinus. In the International Star Registry, housed in a vault in Switzerland, the star Delphinus 20h17m18s12d30'40", magnitude 11.3, was named, at our request, TriLumina: Star of Ancient Wisdom and Love. The name is also listed in a book, *Your Place in the Cosmos, Volume V.*

Lest we sound too much like the businessman in Saint-Exupery's *Little Prince*, who said he owned the stars, "because nobody else before me ever thought of owning them,"[28] Sue and I thrilled to think of personalizing and naming just one star in our shared universe, to symbolize our friendship and our collaborative work together.

We chose the name TriLumina, which, for us, meant "one plus one equals three." While not mathematically correct, we found that when the two of us created workshops together, a "tripling" seemed to happen—our ideas seemed more nuanced and creative than what we might have produced alone. Our workshops, and, later, our guided trips with our friend Trisha focused on ancient wisdom and love. Those were special years. In a sense, we felt guided by our star.

I think now about the different constellations of family and friends in my life, the various ways we have come together, each an individual, and yet forming a constellation larger than ourselves. It does my soul good to wake in the middle of the night, when the stars appear brighter, to absorb the wonder of a constellated sky. It also does my soul good to wake in the middle of the night, when the veils are thinner, to commune not only with the stars, but with loved ones, seen and unseen.

I have never forgotten a young girl who lost her grandfather. She turned to me and pointed to a star in the night sky. "See that star, right there?" she asked. "That's my grandpa."

We were both quiet, watching him twinkle from below.

If you should wake often in the middle of the night, I would tell my younger self, instead of worrying or fretting, make friends with the night. Slip outside and raise your eyes toward the heavens, bedazzled with billions of stars; it is the loveliest look at infinity we, as humans, will ever see. Name some stars, let them guide you. Though they may be light-years away, they can touch your life in untold ways.

And, maybe, just maybe, the tap on your shoulder at 3:00 a.m. does come from a departed loved one, a raven-haired mother or a star-dancing sister, encouraging you to ponder, in the deep stillness of night, what a marvel it is to share a constellation in this lifetime.

Still wrapped in the blanket of night, my eyes loosen their focus on the light-years between me and the stars; I yawn and feel the pull of slumber once more. Pulling the slider closed behind me, I snuggle into the covers beside my quietly puffing husband, another point of light in my universe, the outer star of Orion's belt.

EIGHT FEET, FOUR INCHES

J im and I have only this evening, during sunset, to finish marking my henge on the balcony. Otherwise we will have to wait an entire year for this exact moment to reoccur. Today, June 21, marks the summer solstice in the Northern Hemisphere.

I cheerfully ferret out a magic marker, hidden beneath a pot holder and a stash of pens and pencils squirreled away in the kitchen drawer. Then I retrieve the tape measure from Jim's toolbox. My measurements will be imprecise and unorthodox; I know this. However, I'm determined to mark off a henge on our balcony. Hopefully, no clouds will obscure the horizon.

"What exactly is a henge?" Jim had asked, peeling his breakfast banana six months earlier. The sweet smell of ripe banana filled the space between us.

"Well," I began, idly circling cubes of ice in my morning glass of iced tea. "You're familiar with Stonehenge."

Jim scrunched his eyebrows, his puzzled look translating into wary uncertainty, something akin to, *Surely you don't intend to build a stone circle on our balcony, do you?*

I have seen this bewildered look on his face countless times during our marriage; he, the pragmatist, is never quite sure what I, the nonpragmatist, will take it upon myself to do next. Even though he doesn't share, nor totally understand, my desire to unravel and explore more nontraditional endeavors, he rarely stands in my way and, even more often, takes a certain pride in my undertakings. Our differences blend in a harmonious way. I am his wings and he is my anchor. So, it is with genuine interest that he wants to try and understand what I want to do.

"A lot of places like Stonehenge," I continued, "were astronomically aligned to track the movement of the sun during the year, like the winter and summer solstices."

Jim folded his banana peel and placed it neatly on his napkin, waiting for me to continue, the spark of understanding not yet ignited in his eyes.

"My definition of a henge is anything that marks the sun's journey across the sky, or the moon's journey, for that matter—it can be a stone pillar, a monument, or, in my case, two specific slats on our balcony rail."

I pointed to the bay windows in the kitchen where we sat. "You know how, in the winter, we can see the sun set in that window to the south, and how, in the summer, the sun moves farther north and we see it set through that window?" (We both know the sun's movement is an illusion, caused by the tilt of the earth's axis. But, from the vantage point of Earth, the fixed sun appears to traverse back and forth across the horizon.) Jim nodded thoughtfully.

I want to mark the two days of the year when the sun appears to stand still—the summer and winter solstices. *Solstitium*, a Latin word meaning "sun standing still," refers to the brief pause when the sun appears to reach its most extreme point on the horizon before reversing its direction.

My plan, put simply, is to mark those two extreme points on the horizon as I experience them from my balcony. My henge will be nothing more than marking an x on two different slats on our balcony rail. From the vantage point of my chair, the setting sun on the winter solstice will be behind a different rail than the setting sun on the summer solstice. I want to measure the distance between the two rails.

"Why?" Jim had asked earnestly.

A fair enough question, but slightly harder to answer. "It's just a way for me to track the sun's movement across the horizon, rail by rail, from the shortest to the longest day and back again. And I'm just curious about the distance."

My explanation, however, reflected only the tip of the iceberg. My desire runs much, much deeper.

Jim, my rock and anchor, has never joined me on what I call my archaeological forays to different henges around the world. I have visited a number of stone circles, cairns, and upright pillars, constructed during the Neolithic period, that mark the solstices and equinoxes. I have taken these particular trips with girlfriends or with Mandy.

For as long as I can remember, I have been fascinated with the sky and our relationship to the vast universe beyond. Learning the machinations of the moon and sun make me feel as if I'm discovering the meaning of some exciting and ancient hieroglyphic. I have felt both wonderment and connection as I stood among the monoliths of Stonehenge in England, in early morning, dew dampening my boots, as I circled the silent stones, which are astronomically aligned to create an observatory of sorts.

I felt like a time traveler crossing the Gulf of Morbihan in Brittany; our boat sliced through misty waters as we motored toward the uninhabited island of Gavrinis. Entering a large cairn, carved with patterns and symbols, I stood within inches of ancient multiton slabs of stone, chiseled with hundreds of magnificent swirls inside a chamber that welcomed the passage of the winter solstice sun creeping along its walls.

In County Meath, Ireland, Mandy and I stood breathless, shoulder to shoulder, in thick, velvet-black darkness in the passageway of Newgrange, a monument predating the pyramids. Waiting in hushed silence inside the mysterious inner chamber, Mandy and I witnessed an amazing demonstration. We saw how the first rays of the rising sun, on the winter solstice, penetrate a roof box. The sun sends a beam of winter light crawling along a darkened sixty-two-foot corridor, which is precisely aligned so that the solstice sun slowly illuminates a dramatic triple spiral, carved into the wall of the womb-like interior. Greatly moved by that experience, I purchased a small replica of that triple spiral, which now lives on my office shelf.

Mandy and I also traced the path of the autumn equinox to a dolmen in Carrowmore near Sligo, Ireland, and, in the company of an archaeologist, we explored the astronomically aligned pueblos of Chaco Canyon in our own American Southwest. The alignments of Chaco remained unknown until 1977, when it was noticed, quite by accident, that a ray of light on the summer solstice penetrated an interior darkness and lit up a single spiral, carved into the rock face of a bluff called Fajada Butte. The rediscovery of this astronomical marker, known as the Sun Dagger, has led to research showing that many of the Chaco pueblos mark the movements of the moon and sun.[29] I remember as a child, growing up in the Southwest, how drawn I felt to these types of ruins. Perhaps, on some level, I sensed their astronomical connection with the moon, sun, and stars.

Modern monuments, too, have been designed to align with the movement of the sun. Less than an hour away from Mandy and Jared's house in Arizona, the Anthem Veterans Memorial dedicated on November 11, 2011, honors the service and sacrifice of our armed forces. Every year, at exactly 11:11 a.m. on November 11, hundreds of people gather to witness the sun's rays shining through the ellipses of the five armed services pillars, which form a perfect solar spotlight over a glass mosaic of the Great Seal of the United States. This happens only one day a year, on Veterans Day.[30]

I have no doubt that the monuments of old held as much meaning, significance, and symbolism as the Anthem Veterans Memorial. The exactitude and precision of all these monuments, passageways, and dwellings inspires awe. In essence, these places are sacred, three-dimensional calendars, inviting the sky to join the earth in a celestial dance of life and seasons.

Never content to be a wallflower, I long to join this dance. I want to twine with the sky. I want to recognize and familiarize myself with the movements of the universe, tilting first toward the sun and then away, moving to the eternal rhythm of existence. I want to lift my eyes, throw open my heart, and offer up my hand. And, yes, just for my own amusement, I want to measure the distance the sun travels between two slats, here, on my balcony rail, on my small barrier island at the edge of the sea.

Standing barefoot now, on the cool tile of the balcony, waiting for the summer solstice sunset, I have no megalithic stones or dolmens for my henge. I have only my permanent marker and our sea-green balcony rail, spanning the distance between two stuccoed titan pillars that support the balcony roof over my head. The placement of these two titan pillars, unlike Stonehenge or Newgrange, has nothing to do with the sun's passage across the horizon, nor were they meant to signal the lengthening or shortening of days. However, after being held captive by a thousand wondrous sunsets on this very balcony, I have observed, between the titans, the sun's yearly trek from south to north and back again.

In the winter, during the shortening of days, the sun takes its bow closer to the rails of the southern pillar on my left, and, on the lengthening of days, it sidesteps a number of rails north, toward the pillar on my right.

Six months ago, on the winter solstice, Jim and I lined up the setting sun behind the fifth slat on the balcony rail near the southern titan pillar and marked it with an *x*. I have been waiting, since then, to count how many slats the sun travels north.

Jim has agreed to help me again. In fact, he's quite on board this time. Good with all things numeral (if he hadn't memorized my telephone number more than fifty years ago, we would not be together today), he commandeers his watch, the permanent marker, and the measuring tape.

To be more precise, we align the leg of my wicker chair on the corner of a specific tile, making sure to situate it on the exact spot where I sat when I watched the setting sun disappear during the winter solstice six months earlier.

Satisfied, I settle onto the cushion and wait for the summer sun to bow and disappear, as the Northern Hemisphere bids farewell to the longest day of the year. The sky begins to blush as the sun greets the sea; no cloud bank obstructs our view. I am reminded of a curtain call, that moment just before the applause begins. It warrants a standing ovation, actually, the sun's completion of its six-month journey north.

And then, quietly, it disappears—a fiery ball melting into the sea. The days of lengthening light have come to a cosmic standstill!

Jim cocks his wrist and looks at his watch. "Eight twenty-one," he announces.

I point to the slat that marked the place where the sun disappeared, from my vantage point on the chair.

"There. Right there," I say, pointing.

We count. It's the twenty-eighth slat on the balcony rail.

"You sure?" Jim asks, pulling off the cap of the permanent marker, a waft of solvent permeating the air.

"I'm sure."

He marks the underside of the rail with an *x*.

We now have our two points of reference; we can measure the distance between slats five and twenty-eight. Jim unwinds his tape measure, the tinny scrape of aluminum sliding across the metal rail. He is precise, just like the builders of old. Precision required them to maneuver multiton boulders within fractions of an inch, allowing one ray of sunlight or moonlight, at a precise hour, on a precise day, to travel down a dark passageway and light up an inner chamber.

Jim stoops to read the numbers on the tape measure.

Eight feet and...how many inches? Four, yes, four inches; he's sure of it. The distance between the solstices, in our small corner of the world, measures eight feet, four inches.

Tomorrow, the sun begins its return journey south, toward the equator, toward the standing pillar to my left, toward the fifth slat on our balcony rail.

Unlike my ancestors, I have no need of a sacred, three-dimensional calendar to discern the best time to sow and reap, or to mark the return of more light-filled days, but I yearn, nonetheless, to align myself with the rhythms of the cosmos, to mark my earthly crosshairs within its vastness. My simple henge connects me to the great celestial dance of seasons; it connects me to the solstices of the passing years; and it creates a reference point, a thread, connecting me to the earth's year-long journey around the sun, marked inch by inch upon my balcony rail.

Seasons and solstices imitate life, I would tell my younger self. "To every thing there is a season . . . a time to be born, and a time to die; a time to plant, and a time to pluck up that which is planted . . . a time to weep, and a time to laugh; a time to mourn, and a time to dance." Ecclesiastes 3:1-4 [31]

From birth to death, we participate in the ebb-and-flow rhythm of the great cosmic dance. What a gift to be invited to this dance, to live a life. Dark seasons will descend, yes, but remember, too, they will pass, traversing across your corner of the world toward the promise of more light-filled days. Weather winter's darkness, rejoice in spring's beginnings, revel in summer's light, and harvest autumn's bounty. Don't futilely cling to one season or another; rather, allow them to cycle through you, over and over. Celebrate your journey around the

*sun. Make a henge. Invite the sky to earth. Dance. Fan the flame
of awe. Allow light to travel down a dark passageway and illumine
a chamber of your soul.*

*From our mortal vantage point, we may not realize that the soul,
like the sun, remains fixed. It does not disappear. It merely appears
to traverse a lifetime across the horizon, rail by rail, year by year,
between the titans of birth and death.*

I open my hand toward Jim. "Want to dance on the summer
solstice?"

He raises his brown eyes and searches mine.

"It only comes around once a year," I add.

He sees I'm serious. With some effort, he pushes himself
up from his chair and takes my hand. In silence, the measuring tape our only witness, my wings fold around his anchor;
we sway together there, in the afterglow of sunset.

KEY MARCO CAT

I have been waiting to make her acquaintance.

Seeing the carved graceful curves of this petite, six-inch feline—part human, part cat—one would think it was a representation of the goddess Bast or Sekhmet, dug up in the sands of Egypt, not far from the Nile. In reality, its origin lies not five miles from me, on the northern end of our island. Anthropologist Frank Cushing discovered it in 1896, buried in the muck and mud of a pond near a shell mound, accompanied by vibrantly colored ceremonial masks and other carved objects.

These rare wooden artifacts, one of the greatest discoveries in the history of North American archaeology, date from 500 BCE to 1500 BCE.[32] Their creators were the Calusa, an artistic tribe inhabiting our island prior to Ponce de León's visit in 1513, when he named our state Florida, a Spanish word meaning *full of flowers*.

I press my forehead to the climate-controlled glass and concrete enclosure, constructed for this very exhibit. The cat woman, carved from native cypress and forever immortalized on a 1989 postage stamp, exemplifies some of the finest pre-Columbian art in North America. She has been housed in the Smithsonian since her discovery by Cushing, but she has come home to our newly finished museum for an extended visit. The hushed tones of visitors and the low light add to her mystery. Her carved eyes are open; she has witnessed centuries. What stories lie trapped within her?

Artifacts and archaeological digs mesmerize me. Veritable time machines, they offer a three-dimensional view of history. Ancient hands, coursing with the DNA of humanity, fashioned wood, clay, and stone into items that served another time and culture. These artifacts evoke in me a kind of *participation mystique*, a phrase coined by French anthropologist Lucien Lévy-Bruhl to describe the feeling of merging with a larger whole, beyond the boundaries of our limited self.

Trying to step into the world of the Calusa, I imagine myself as the carver of the Key Marco Cat. I have uncovered a particularly solid cypress branch, good for carving; it feels smooth and substantial in my palm. Fascinated by the sleek, tawny panthers that swim and hunt in the dense brush surrounding my village, I decide to carve a talisman as protection from their fierceness. When sitting on its haunches, the panther looks like a beautiful woman kneeling. I carve a panther head, etching sun petals around its eyes, and then I carve a woman's body, with a long, graceful panther tail rising the length of her spine. My six-inch carving—part human, part cat—is my gift to the wood, to my village, and to the panther. May all be well. May we live in harmony.

Fast-forwarding to the twenty-first century, it is becoming more difficult to live in harmony. Endangered, only 120 to 130 panthers remain in Florida.[33] They face an uncertain future as development encroaches upon their habitat. I purchased a specialty license plate that reads "Protect the Panther," which contributes to programs to protect panthers. In addition, the National Wildlife Refuge conserves nearly twenty-seven thousand acres for the primary purpose of protecting the Florida panther and its habitat.

The panther-like Key Marco Cat harkens back to a time when panthers were plentiful. I bought a clay replica sculpture of the Key Marco Cat in the early '80s, not long after schoolchildren from Florida voted the panther as the state animal. My sculpture represents the history of our island; she symbolizes mystery and mastery. Her steady presence, like a talisman, evokes well-being: may all be well. May we live in harmony. May beauty dwell within.

Honor that which has come before you, I would tell my younger self. Don't assume that you are "above" Indigenous cultures or that modern society supersedes antiquity. Much wisdom and connection to the earth has been lost in modernity. Participate in the mystery and mystique of those who came before us. Allow your mind to time travel. Imagine witnessing passing centuries; become a sleek cat-woman carving, encased in glass and concrete, looking out through sun-petaled eyes at a woman, grayed at the temples, paying homage to you.

Another group approaches, seeking a glimpse of the six inches of carved cypress. The cat's mystique continues;

the roomful of twenty-first-century humans, many with cell phones, falls silent. A line forms in front of the glass enclosure.

Could her carver ever have imagined this?

TURTLE LADY

I see her, driving her red four-wheeler along the shore at dawn, looking for drag marks. It's nesting season for the loggerhead sea turtle, the world's largest hard-shelled turtle. The Turtle Lady, as we call her, combs the beach from May through October, looking for newly laid nests and, later, for hatchlings attempting to return to the sea.

This morning, she hops off her four-wheeler, grabs a handful of stakes, and pounds them into the sand above the high-tide line. She has spotted a new nest, which she marks off by stringing caution tape around the stakes and affixing the following sign—a stern warning—meant to protect the endangered loggerhead.

Do Not Disturb
Sea Turtle Nest
Violators Subject to Fines and Imprisonment

Florida Law Chapter 370
No person may take, possess, disturb, mutilate, destroy,

cause to be destroyed, sell, offer for sale, transfer, molest, or harass any marine turtle or its nest or eggs at any time.

Upon conviction, a person may be imprisoned for a period of up to 60 days or fined up to $500, or both, plus an additional $100 for each sea turtle egg destroyed or taken.

US Endangered Species Act of 1973
No person may take, harass, harm, pursue, hunt, shoot, wound, kill, trap, or capture any marine turtle, turtle nest, and/or eggs, or attempt to engage in any such conduct.

Any person who knowingly violates any provision of this act may be assessed a civil penalty up to $25,000 or a criminal penalty up to $100,000 and up to one year imprisonment.

Should you witness a violation, action, observe an injured or stranded turtle, or disoriented hatchlings, please contact Florida Fish and Wildlife Commission Marine Turtle Protection Program

These signs, posted at every nest, can number as many as eighty on this four-mile stretch of beach. Our sea turtle protection ordinance requires those of us living along the shore to minimize our artificial lights after 9:00 p.m. during turtle season, by pulling down shades indoors and installing yellow lights outdoors. Sea turtles follow the reflection of moonlight and starlight on the water. Artificial lights can disorient females trying to lay a clutch of eggs and disorient hatchlings from reaching the sea, which means they fall prey to exhaustion, dehydration, fire ants, birds, and ghost crabs. The abysmal odds for hatchlings to survive to maturity astound me; only an estimated one in one thousand to one in ten thousand reaches adulthood.[34] Once they do mature, however, adult loggerheads can live up to one hundred years.

Later in the summer, around dusk, I see Turtle Lady again at the water's edge, near a nest where one of her volunteers, days earlier, had knelt, taken out a stethoscope, and bent to listen for movement in the egg chamber beneath the sand. A stethoscope, positioned on top of a soon-to-hatch nest, will magnify the sounds of turtles hatching en masse and scrabbling upward toward the surface. With enough notice, the volunteers sometimes create a makeshift path from the nest toward the open water, to help the hatchlings find their way into the sea.

However, Turtle Lady does not have a stethoscope this evening; instead, she carries a bucket. I suck in my breath when I guess the contents. I approach quietly, and sure enough, she reaches in, removes a hatchling, and positions it upon the wet sand. Without hesitation, the hatchling scrambles toward the foamy water.

I stand there, transfixed, wanting to help but daring not to interfere; I have read the warning signs many times. Turtle Lady studies my face. She knows the answer before she asks, "Would you like to release one?"

My hands touch my heart. "Oh, could I?" I cup my palms toward her, as if receiving communion. She offers me a sand-crusted baby loggerhead, whose shell is no larger than a silver dollar.

"Some of them became disoriented," she explains. "I found them in the dunes."

The hatchling's wind-milling flippers tickle my palms. I am holding one of nature's creations, a perfect miniature of a magnificent loggerhead. A massive journey awaits this little critter. Ever so gently, I lower it onto the sand and offer it like a gift to the sea.

If female, upon reaching sexual maturity, she will return to this nesting beach, even if thirty years have passed, to lay her own clutch of eggs.[35] If male, he will never again leave the water. The sand temperature during incubation influences a turtle's sex. I surmise that my turtle is female because the past two months have been particularly warm.

I watch her windmill her miniature flippers into the surf and disappear. I am in awe of her homing instinct. May your journey be safe, I say inwardly, and may you be the one in a thousand to return here, someday, to this very shore.

Protect the wild and endangered in the world, I would tell my younger self. But also protect the wild and endangered within you. Mark a sacred space for yourself; do not let others tread upon the hallowed ground where your ideas and creativity gestate. Raise a protective shield as you patiently wait and listen for stirrings within. When the time comes to bring something forth into the world, don't be disoriented by someone else's candle or flame, no matter how brightly it shines. Follow the light of your own true path; let all else fall by the wayside. For here, upon this familiar shore of your hatching, you can return, time and time again, to create anew.

At home, after dinner, just before I close the shutters to block the light from our chandelier, I pause, looking out into the dark water. Somewhere out there, a tiny loggerhead forges her way in the sea.

GRANDMOTHER MOON

Well after midnight, 1:00 a.m. to be exact.

Mandy and I tug our beach chairs into an open clearing and plop two heavy throws on top of them. The waves lap less than one hundred feet away, yet Mandy and I look outfitted to ski down the slopes of the Rocky Mountains. In addition to my ski parka, I wear long underwear, a wool hat, gloves, a turtleneck, and thick woolen socks. Mandy, who has the slim figure of a runner, resembles a padded hockey player, ready to tackle the ice.

Not surprisingly, we're alone on this frigid, especially for Florida, night. Unbeknownst to us, we're in the midst of the coldest December on record. Undeterred, Mandy and I excitedly burrow beneath the blankets, leaving only our noses exposed to breathe and our eyes free to stare into the heavens.

"We're crazy," I say to Mandy.

"I love it," she giggles.

"We won't be around for the next one," I tease.

Mandy's teeth glisten in the moonlight. I treasure these times and feel blessed to call her my daughter and my best friend. She loves adventures as much as I do, maybe more. She often takes over where I leave off.

"Thanks for talking me into staying up all night," I add.

She lifts her head. "Seriously?"

"Seriously."

I mean it, even though I'm an early-to-bed and early-to-rise person: I have not pulled an all-nighter since Mandy's childhood. And then only because her chicken pox erupted in the worst imaginable places; her sole relief had been hourly oatmeal baths.

But tonight our vigil has nothing to do with chicken pox. We have come, instead, to watch and pay homage to the lunar eclipse. Not just any lunar eclipse, but a rare one. Today marks the winter solstice.

The last full-moon total lunar eclipse on the winter solstice happened in 1638. That was the same year spiritual leader and midwife Anne Hutchinson, regarded as one of the earliest American feminists,[36] was banned from the Massachusetts Bay Colony for her religious beliefs and for challenging male authority.

I delight in thinking that Anne may have watched that 1638 eclipse, watched this very moon turning a coppery orange outside her new home in what is now Portsmouth, Rhode Island. Anne, who read widely and thought deeply, not only birthed babies; she helped birth the idea that daughters, like the precious jewel lying on the chaise beside me, deserve to be on equal footing with men.

What an audacious idea!

I feel an invisible thread tying Mandy and me to Anne,

and to all women, especially those who, like us, venture from their comfortable beds to behold the moon. Women have been associated with the moon since the beginning of time. The moon's monthly cycle and women's menstrual cycles mimic one another. In some Indigenous cultures, the term *moontime* means a woman's menstrual cycle.

Many cultures refer to the moon as female; her face, outlined within the lunar seas, governs the rise and fall of ocean tides. She has been known as Grandmother Moon, Selene, Artemis, Chang'e, and numerous other names. Louisa May Alcott wrote about Mother Moon, and Greek poet Sappho, born in 615 BCE, wrote, "When, round and full, her silver face, swims into sight, and lights all space." The next time Grandmother Moon's full silver face will be completely veiled on the winter solstice will be December 21, 2094. If I possessed a grandmother–Methuselah gene, I would be 145 years old.

What strides will transpire in the decades between now and then? NASA's Artemis program hopes to land a woman on the moon by 2024. What new audacious thoughts will be born? Whatever transpires between now and then, a new earth audience will gather to watch what Mandy and I see now.

1:33 a.m.

Mandy points skyward. The earth's faint shadow, or penumbra, has taken its first bite of the moon. Mandy and I reminisce about the many times we have looked up into the night sky: the time we vacationed in Telluride and studied the white cloud of the Milky Way; the time a family friend set up a telescope in an open field behind our house to show us the rings that encircle Saturn and the moon's dry seas; the time we lay in the bed of a pickup truck and watched meteors streak the sky; and the time we stared, openmouthed, at the dwarf galaxies of the Magellanic Clouds in the Maasai Mara game preserve as lions roared not far away.

2:41 a.m.

We lie on our backs and watch the earth's shadow swallow the entire moon. I adjust the afghan more snugly around me. I tell Mandy about the time my dad woke me from sleep to lead me outside, barefoot and still in my pajamas. He pointed to the sky to show me the planet Venus kissing the crescent moon, a memory still warm after sixty-four years. The strongest fiber of that memory, however, is not what I saw, but how I felt, standing there, looking up into the sky and then back at Daddy's face, flush with awe and love.

I believe this night, too, will lie in Mandy's memory like an ember, fanned to flame someday in the future, when her face is upturned toward the sky.

3:17 a.m.

The umbra, the dark center of the earth's shadow, creates an eerie orange-red glow. We both ooh and ahh.

"I wouldn't have missed this for anything," Mandy says.

"Me neither," I answer, tugging my hat back over one ear.

The moon looks smudged, like a giant eraser has tried to erase it from the sky. It's easy to understand why early cultures worried about Grandmother Moon during an eclipse, her bright white face sullied and dimmed. To help her heal, some sang songs; others beat drums and pots to ward off whatever threatened to devour her completely.

I can relate to their fear on some level. When the world's darkness and sadness eclipse its light and joy, I despair about our future. When the bright face of hope sullies and dims, I become alarmed. What can be done? Is there some greater force at work? I have no idea. In the meantime, maybe singing songs and beating drums keeps hope alive in the heart.

5:01 a.m.

The moon gleams bright white once again. Our vigil draws to a close. I yawn, raise my stiff body off the lounge, and squeeze Mandy's hand. We gather up our covers and see a light flick on in an early riser's window.

5:30 a.m.

Mandy butters toast while I crack two eggs into a sizzling skillet. We agree that this night is a memory maker, something we will recall the rest of our lives.

"I'm not sure what I did to deserve you," I tell Mandy as we clean up.

She argues that she is the lucky one.

"You are the moon in my sky," I whisper as I hug her good night.

"You are the moon in mine," she echoes, padding toward the guest room.

This I know. She will take over where I leave off.

6:30 a.m.

I change into my pajamas, crawl quietly into bed beside Jim, and surrender to sleep.

Be a memory maker, I would tell my younger self. Memories don't depend on fancy vacations halfway around the world. They can be quiet, simple moments, deeply embraced, like witnessing an eclipse, something humans have done since the beginning of time.

Bundle up and make a date with the universe and Grandmother Moon. Spend a night with your eyes and heart wide-open, staring into the heavens, light-years away. Experience the grandeur and wonder, not only of a rare eclipse, but of a rare opportunity, to be fully present with someone you love—even if it means staying up all night. Experiencing a celestial event, cooking an early-morning breakfast, crawling into bed at dawn—moments such as these burrow themselves deeply into the heart. They remain there, untouched by time, shining. Always shining.

11:35 a.m.

I rouse, groggily, and then smile, remembering.

BROKEN CLAMSHELLS

A young brother and sister bolt past me, their footsteps slapping the shore as they giggle and try to outrun one another. Just as abruptly, they halt in front of a cache of shells and beach drift washed up by the tide. Turning and pointing toward the pile, they yell, "Look, Mommy. Shells."

Their mother, her beach cover-up billowing in the wind, holds up her shelling bag and smiles as she walks toward them.

The children have indeed found the mother lode for shelling. The tides, of late, have washed up some nice specimens in this very area. Even though I have at least a thousand shells ferreted away in bowls, cases, and shelves, just yesterday I succumbed and picked up a few more shells from this spot—a shiny, lettered olive and a limpet, one of Mandy's favorites, because it looks like a conical Asian hat with a hole in the top.

The brother and sister squat and noisily rake through the table of shells, set by the sea. I, too, stop. I'm curious.

What types of shells will attract these young beachcombers; possibly the cylindrical left-handed lightning whelk, sitting atop the pile? Most univalves spiral to the right, but lightning whelks, evidently missing that particular evolutionary memo, spiral counterclockwise. I also spot an alphabet cone, so called because letters of the English alphabet can be found in their unique markings.

Actually, I am tempted to reach in and snatch up the alphabet cone; they're harder to come by. But I don't want to be an interloper. We shell collectors can get rather territorial at times. I'm reminded of our seagulls that huff, fluff up their feathers, and squawk noisily to ward off other birds. Considerate shell collectors practice social distancing, so I keep my distance. Truthfully, though, I might not be so magnanimous if I really needed that alphabet cone for my collection. Or, if I were to see, say, a large, orange lion's paw, which I covet to find someday—I might start posturing and puffing up my chest.

However, the young beachcombers' criteria seem much different from my own.

The young girl triumphantly holds up a broken clamshell, evidently enamored with either its salty whiteness or its unique, jagged shape. Her choice amuses me. Small white clamshells litter this beach by the tens of thousands; they are plain, plentiful, and ordinary, the most mundane of all shells. I have not bothered, even, to add them to my collection.

The older brother studies his sister's shell and then reaches into the pile. "Here's another one," he says, handing her the shell.

By the time their mom catches up with them, they have

gathered up fistfuls of shells, most of them clams, many of them chipped and broken. With outstretched hands, they offer up their bounty.

"Oh my," the mother exclaims, examining and fussing over their treasures. She could not be more complimentary if every single shell were a lion's paw instead of a clam. She opens the shelling bag as wide as her heart, inviting the children to drop their shells inside, which they do.

After the children hug their mother's waist, I watch the three of them grow smaller as they continue their walk on the beach, their shelling bag swinging to and fro. In time, their gathered shells may be misplaced, outgrown, or forgotten, but something more important will linger. I can see it in the children's squared shoulders, the way they break into a run again and then look back toward their mother. Their ability to find beauty in the broken clam far outweighs any other treasure they could have found.

Lingering there, I wonder what I overlook along the shoreline of my own life. Where do I fail to see beauty and value? What about the homeless man at the intersection, holding up his scribbled sign: *Anything you can spare is appreciated.* Do I value him as much as the two young children walking down the beach with their mother? What about migrant workers, or workers in a mine or an oil field? Are their eight-, ten-, twelve-hour days valued as much as those spent behind a desk? Certainly the answer to these questions should be an unequivocal *yes*.

What about my own mother? Did I value her as much as I valued the June Cleaver mothers or the mother who just oohed and aahed over her children's broken clamshells?

Childhood memories parade across my mind. By the

time I was twelve, Mama put me in charge of taking care of my five younger sisters. I often wondered where Mama was and when she might return home. Sometimes the responsibility felt crushing. But the titanic bond I forged with my sisters is indestructible; it has blessed me for a lifetime. Mama is the one who gave us to each other. I think Mama did the best she could, considering her own upbringing, and I believe she loved every one of us. She told me that she used to hold my hand through the slats of my crib to help me sleep. Therein lies the beauty in brokenness.

Value can be found in the ordinary and broken places as well as the exceptional, I would tell my younger self. If we soften our gaze and refocus, not on past transgressions, assumptions, or judgments, but on the hands that reach out —holding a sign, a bushel basket, a pick, or a baby's hand—we may startle to find value and beauty where we failed to see it before.

The extraordinary is often tucked within the folds of the ordinary. If we fail to find value and beauty, we miss a thousand opportunities to marvel—for most of life takes place in unremarkable moments. If a broken or undervalued piece of the world lies at your fingertips, reach through the slats that divide, hold it close, and look upon it with new eyes. Value what is, what was, and what might yet be.

I kneel beside the pile of shells, picking up a broken clam. I rub the rough ribs between my fingertips. The ocean has carved the vanilla-white shell into the shape of a cloud. I slip it into my pocket. It may well be one of my more valuable finds.

THE GIFT OF DAYS

Writing on my iPad, table-side, beneath the thatched roof of my favorite restaurant, I kid the waitress that I may have to pay rent. She waves away my comment and sets down a second weeping glass of club soda capped with a wedge of lemon. It's off-season and no one minds that I linger after lunch to write in this Bohemian haunt, something I imagine Hemingway might have liked—open-aired and on the water. A rusted fan attached to a nearby pole lulls me with its hypnotic hum, and fingers of air stir my bangs.

This languid afternoon feeds my soul, oozing in and around me, like the delectable sauce, earlier, that smothered my shrimp tacos and dripped down my fingertips. Settling into seventy, I have more appetite for these types of days. My heavily notated, regimented, and jam-packed calendar has given way to more white spaces, filled with more afternoons such as this, open to eddies of time, allowing me to ponder, observe, and write.

A day such as this fills my inner well to overflowing.

The gift of it, wrapped in the present moment, delights me with its simplicity and potency. I value this gift so much that I have even named it; I call it the Gift of a Day.

Mandy and I have given each other the gift of a day numerous times over the years. When we set out, we have no goal to reach a particular destination in mind. We simply make a pact to be fully present to one another, put away our cell phones, and raise our antennae for nudges, such as: turn down this street, see what's around that corner, or let's just sit here for a while and take in that red-tailed hawk, perched on that tree limb.

When I was a younger woman, my self-worth hinged more on output than process. Being the daughter of a mother who married six times and who rarely participated in any parental activities at school, I vowed to be the best mom and wife I could possibly be. I gave little thought to being the best me. I sewed pillows, curtains, pajamas, dozens of costumes, even a smoking jacket for Jim, who doesn't smoke. I baked my own bread, canned applesauce and salsa, and took microwave cooking classes where I blew up a number of gooey eggs trying to be inventive. I decorated cakes and handmade Christmas gifts. I volunteered to be room mom, team mom, and a chaperone for most every field trip. I taught vacation Bible school, became an elder at church, a Stephen minister, and a youth group leader. In my spare time, I went back to school, acquired a master's degree, and wrote books and articles that were, ironically, mainly about soulfulness and process.

No wonder I began to feel depleted instead of nourished. The sheer number of these worthwhile projects was unsustainable. The vast reservoir of my creativity, passion, and devotion dropped to an alarmingly low level. Trying to regain some balance, I started to incorporate respites from the busyness of life—these respites gave birth to my Gift of a Day idea. What better legacy to leave my daughter than days devoted to the life-giving waters of soulfulness and being?

I am also blessed with three dear friends familiar with the idea of giving the gift of a day. For the past sixteen years, Sue, Trisha, Curly, and I, all living in different parts of the country, have set aside six days—two days for travel and four gift days, one for each of us—to tuck away our cell phones, be fully present, and *listen* one another into being. To be given an entire day to bask in the undivided attention of these wise, supportive women has been life-changing.

In addition to listening one another into being, we witness, brainstorm, give feedback, receive, encourage, and celebrate. Each one of us chooses one day to be *our* day. On our particular day, we are in charge and can use the day however we wish. We tell the other three what we need from our day, what time we'll meet, and when and where we'll eat. No two days look alike, and all of our days change from year to year.

When a question arises about what to do, we look to the recipient of the day, lift our shoulders, and reply in unison, "It's your day!"

Almost all of us choose to sit in a circle and talk for at least a portion of our day; the gift of rapt attention for creative projects, upcoming milestones, and life changes nurtures and sustains us. In addition to our priceless circle time, we may include another activity. Curly, our textile artist, has taken us to several art exhibits; Trisha, our travel diva and guide, has included slides from around the world as well as several museum visits; Sue, our author, took us to the obscure house where two of her historical fiction characters actually lived.

Everyone's day broadens my horizons and bears its gifts. I am the better for their sharing. But I also love the opportunity to share what lies in my heart at its deepest core. Sue, Trisha, and Curly have witnessed my journey and ripening. Sue, longer than the others, has walked steadfastly beside me for decades. The gift of a day shared with these remarkable women has enriched me beyond compare.

In addition to their untold influence, these girlfriends have brainstormed book ideas with me, listened to me read, helped interpret my dreams, consoled me after my sister Nancy's death, joined me on a creative visualization, given me feedback on an international project, taken a lazy afternoon raft ride (lashed together) down a river, and, yes, even dressed me in a shower curtain (the closest they could come to a cape) to act out a duel with self-doubt.

To the outside world, wearing a shower curtain and raising your arms in victory might be cause for concern. But to my girlfriends, cheering and applauding, nothing could have been more apropos; they knew I would return home more emboldened to do the work I wanted to do.

Give yourself the occasional gift of a day, I would tell my younger self. Relish the deliciousness of a languid afternoon to dream, ponder, and imagine. Tuck away your cell phone; don't squander your precious awareness on what others post, not on your day. Rather, let your awareness reveal the sacred vibrating beneath the mundane. Listen to the music of a rusted fan; savor, really savor, the salty goodness of a blackened shrimp taco; feel the coolness of an iced glass in your palm. Lift the hem of time and peek into the eternal now.

And, if you're lucky enough to have a daughter and girlfriends willing to offer you a day of their presence, willing to sit in silence to watch a red-tailed hawk, or willing to lash their raft to yours, clasp them tightly and never let them go. They can immerse you in a profound presence—a vortex of love and possibility—that will nurture what is most true within you.

I continue to sit quietly beneath the thatched roof of the restaurant, listening, the ice melting in my club soda. The fan continues its hum, white clouds billow overhead, and a dragonfly zigzags a path toward the water.

I think back to the time my girlfriends traveled here to this island for one of our gatherings. My day included a long, languid walk along our shore; I believe we are the better for it.

FLOOD TIDE

*The period when the
tidal water rises and
flows toward shore*

Then I walked away, and I did not look back.
I had written my troubles on the sand.
The tide was coming in.

—ARTHUR GORDON[37]

TAKING A LEAP

"I'm going for a walk," I tell Jim and Mandy. Zipping up my fuzzy pink jacket, I hurry up the beach, hoping I'm not too late.

I'm not. Within minutes, overhead I spot, one, two, three, four splashes of color, drifting ever closer. The parachuters have shown up again today. All of my adult life, I have wanted to parachute. I seriously explored the possibility in my twenties until I read about the death of a local jumper whose parachute had not been folded properly. My resolve dampened, but not my desire. After giving birth to Mandy, I would not risk a poorly folded parachute.

However, on one family vacation, I did don a flight suit and helmet, sign a waiver, and step into a vertical wind tunnel. Mandy and Jim watched and waved through the window as I rose into the air and flipped at various angles, depending on how I positioned my arms and legs. I was told this awesome feeling is exactly what skydiving feels like. I couldn't stop smiling. Mandy, only seven and evidently impressed, later pointed to some parachuters at an air show and pronounced loudly, "My mom does that, too." I smiled sheepishly at the raised eyebrows. "Well, not exactly," I added, realizing that a wind tunnel hardly compared to jumping out of an airplane.

A green cloth cloud descends right beside me on the shore. The jumper lightly touches down on the sand and quickly gathers his voluminous chute toward him. The zipping sound of nylon surrounds me as the other parachuters descend in a rainbow of colors. I stand and watch, mesmerized.

"Anyone want to go up with us?" a woman shouts, looking down at her clipboard. "We have room for one more."

My breath catches. How could that be?

"What do you mean?" I ask.

"Well," she says pointing to a tall, blond parachuter, "Roy, here, can take someone tandem with him on our next jump."

"You don't need lessons?" I stammer. Several parachuters from an out-of-town jumping club shake their head no in unison.

The woman sidles up to Roy. "Roy can teach you everything you need to know before we go up. The cost is $125."

I size up Roy. "You've done this before?" I open my beach purse to make sure I threw in my credit card.

"Hundreds of times. Nothing to it." He stretches out his parachute on the dune and begins folding it.

"Am I too old?" I ask, feeling a little self-conscious in my pink fleece jacket.

He looks me over and shakes his head. "Hardly. My oldest client was ninety. His birthday present." Roy seems very methodical and unruffled, the type to take extra care when folding a parachute.

The jumping club begins to gather around me. "Is she going up?" I hear someone ask. "Not sure," someone else answers.

I'm at a crossroads. One arrow points to the sky and an opportunity to do something I've always wanted to do (I wouldn't even miss a single night's sleep fretting about it), and the other arrow points to my two feet, grounded solidly upon the sand. I told Jim and Mandy I would be taking an afternoon walk. But, from somewhere deep within, I know that if I don't jump, quite literally, out of this window, fortuitously opened, I never will. Tellingly, that thought saddens me.

"Okay," I say, sucking in my breath. "I'll do it on one condition. I have to call my husband and daughter. They think I'm taking a walk."

I keep getting a busy signal; Mandy is talking to her college girlfriend. Finally, she answers. My words come tumbling out. I hear her take a deep breath and then the long pause. I am well aware of her protectiveness toward me and my welfare. One of her favorite sayings as a child was always *I want your feet right here on the ground beside me.*

I know it takes a lot for her to say, "You've always wanted to do it, Mom." I think her blessing carries the same trepidation I felt when I blessed her weeks-long treks into the back country with bears and without cell-phone service. Then she adds, with more gusto, "Go for it!"

Jim is less enthusiastic, but he also knows how headstrong I can be once I've made up my mind to do something.

"It's your life," he says, finally, which I know means, *It scares me to think of you doing this.*

The jumping club assures me the most dangerous part of

the whole escapade is driving to the airport. We crowd into a van and head to our one-runway airport, ten miles away. In the van, Roy coaches me on what to do after we jump from the plane: thrust out your chin, keep your forearms raised with your elbows bent near your waist, and pick up your feet when we land. I'm sure he has told me something else, but I have already forgotten.

Once at the airport, Roy cinches me into my harness, way too tightly. The straps dig into my shoulders. "This is a little tight," I say, pointing to the shoulder strap.

"Gotta be," Roy says, yanking on another strap. "I'm the one with the parachute."

My eyebrows raise. Valid point. Perspective is everything. I move around a bit in the harness. "Actually, this might be just a little loose," I say, pointing to the very shoulder strap I thought was too tight just a few moments earlier.

Roy smiles and gives another tug. We're off.

"Did you fold the parachute we're using?" I ask for reassurance, my voice squeakier than normal.

"No, someone else did," Roy says matter-of-factly, as if our well-being has nothing to do with how scrupulously someone else folded our lifeline to earth.

Too late. I am whisked into the small plane with the jumping club. We're climbing to fourteen thousand feet above the island. Pats and encouragement come from some of the jumpers. They must remember the churning in their own stomachs the first time they stepped out of a plane with only a few yards of cloth to break their fall.

I can't see Roy; I can only feel him strapped to my back. My life depends on someone I have known for less than an hour. I hear two of the jumpers at the back of the plane yelling up to the pilot. "A little left. A little more to the right."

My eyes widen at the imprecision of the directions. What happens if we're too far right or left? No time to think. Roy says we're next. We walk crab-like to the threshold of the plane. I look down at the island that has shrunk considerably from fourteen thousand feet above. I am looking DOWN into the hazy-blue sky, not up. All of a sudden, I feel my face pale. I know what *a little to the left or right* means. We could miss the island completely and land in the sea.

Lord, have mercy. What have I gotten myself into?

I feel Roy nudging me forward. I pause there on the threshold of the plane, the solid floor still beneath my feet. Every survival instinct in my cells screams, *Don't jump— you'll die.* I remember a pivotal scene in *Indiana Jones*—Harrison Ford's leap of faith as he steps out into the abyss only to find he does not plunge to his death.

The island looks so small.

I take a deep breath and plunge forward. It is either the bravest or most foolhardy thing I have ever done.

Falling, wind howling in my ears, our velocity approaching 120 miles per hour, I remember to thrust out my chin. My cheeks flap. I raise my forearms like Roy instructed and I feel a cushion of air against my belly. I'm not wearing a sleek jumping suit, like Roy; I am wearing my fuzzy pink jacket, falling through the sky, smiling like the Cheshire cat.

Take the leap, I would tell my younger self. Don't let fear stop you from accomplishing something your soul yearns to experience. Though years may pass, don't give up. Your deep desire to pursue something burns like a flame in the heart. Fan that flame; keep it alive. It may very well light the path for opportunity to knock on your door. The knock may be as innocuous as taking a walk. Recognize the knock when it comes. Invite opportunity in. Say yes, even if it takes your breath away. Especially if it takes your breath away! For that is what epiphanies do.

When Roy pulls the parachute cord, we're yanked upward beneath a canopy of orange. Our hurtling ten-thousand-foot free fall snaps to a halt, and we begin to glide and float in total silence. I feel as free as a frigatebird soaring above the earth. Roy, still at my back, says nothing; he allows me to absorb the magic of this moment without interruption. I can see for miles beyond the bridge of our island, miles down the beach, and miles out into the horizon, where the sun hangs low and has begun dismantling light into tinges of color.

As we descend nearer to the beach, I see Mandy and Jim, their smiling faces turned upward; they are waving. They must recognize my fuzzy pink jacket. Mandy bounces up and down. I wave back.

Roy reviews the landing protocol. Then he steps down onto the soft sand, and my footsteps follow. We touch down with ease, a perfect landing, as if we had practiced a hundred times.

My body alights, but my spirit still soars. "We did it," I tell Roy. He raises his hand in a high five, as do others in the jumping club. Smiles and laughter abound.

Later, after the parachutes have been tucked away and daylight turns to dusk, I walk home arm in arm with Mandy and Jim. In the soft afterglow of sunset, happiness pulses through me like an electrical current. I am overcome with gratefulness for Mandy and Jim—their support, their pride, and, most especially, their feet, right here, on the ground beside me.

VESPERS BY THE SEA

The magic hour is upon us.

Jim pours himself a chardonnay and me a pinot grigio. We open the slider and settle comfortably onto the cushioned patio chairs overlooking the Gulf as the sun prepares to take its final bow. Already, the spectacle has begun; the sky looks like a painter's palette, wells of color spilling, splashing, and blending into yellow, orange, crimson, and mauve swirls.

"Think we'll see a green flash?" I ask Jim as I slip off my sandals.

"We might," he says, setting his drink down on the mosaic table beside our propped-up feet. "There's no cloud bank, and it looks clear enough."

We first heard of the green flash years ago, when we were still new to the island. Since then, we have seen it several hundred times. Unique atmospheric conditions refract the light of the setting sun and cause the uppermost rim of the sun to appear emerald green, just seconds before it disappears below the horizon. It happens so quickly some people refer to it as a wink—Neptune's wink—a name I fancy. I can almost picture Neptune smiling and winking good night.

Wink instead of *flash* more accurately describes what we commonly see, the final farewell of the sun winking into a small green gem and disappearing. Not that a flash is impossible, but an actual flash of green light, streaking like lightning, is much rarer. So rare, in fact, Jim and I have never been lucky enough to see one of these green lightning flashes, except on a video taken at sunset.

"I'll be right back," Jim says, setting down his wineglass and hurrying inside.

I smile. The entire sky blazes with color. I know exactly what will happen next. While I wait, I watch a droplet of condensation slowly glide down the side of Jim's wineglass, glimmering in the sunlight.

Sure enough, Jim returns with his phone in hand, aims, and clicks three, maybe four, photographs. I love how this no-nonsense, logical, do-it-by-the-book man is repeatedly enchanted by the sun's evening performances. He has amassed a nothing-but-sunsets album with countless photographs of spectacular sunsets. His collection has swelled to such size that he reasons he doesn't need any more. And then, sure enough, the sun and sky perform a duet so compelling, he cannot resist.

Tonight is one of those nights.

However, I suspect that tonight's performance has an additional costar as well, all the way from Africa. Saharan dust, guided by the trade winds, often permeates our southern Florida atmosphere, especially in the summer. When present, it acts as a prism, scattering sunlight into dazzling reds and oranges. Ever since I was a young girl, I have been drawn to Africa, and it pleases me to think that a piece of Africa has been drawn to me. Some Saharan dust storms, detectable by satellite, can measure more than a thousand square miles. In a year's time, these storms can hurl over one hundred million tons of dust into the atmosphere and across the Atlantic.[38] Tonight, we are the beneficiaries of African dust, as are others who have gathered below us on the beach to watch the sunset.

Just as the sun dips, we see Neptune wink.

"There it is," Jim and I say in unison.

We hear clapping from below. People often applaud the moment the sun disappears. This end-of-day applause always delights me. Sunsets stir something archetypal within us, connecting us not only with each other, but with nature and the larger circle of life. It's as if we humans understand, on some level, that the setting sun represents an ending, a goodbye, filled not with grief or dread or fear, but only awe.

Paying homage to the day swells my heart. This is why I love our evening ritual. It feels like praying the sun down, much like vespers, the sixth canonical hour for evening prayer. Vesper service includes, among other things, lighting lamps and candles, whereby the day is put away and the night unfurled.

At the end of every day, I would tell my younger self, pause and take in what is happening before your very eyes. It might be as dazzling as a Technicolor sunset, as quick as a green wink, or as quiet as a water droplet sliding down the outside of a glass. Offer gratitude for at least one thing, no matter how small or minute—the sound of people applauding sunset, the presence of two wineglasses instead of one, a man hurrying to get his camera—these are minute sands of gratitude. Compounded, gratitude can travel great heights and distances; it can change the atmosphere of our lives. Gratitude acts like a prism, scattering inconceivable light into our world.

Our empty wineglasses clink as I carry them indoors and click on the lamp that rests on our kitchen counter. For years, I have lighted this stone lamp at dusk. Only now do I recognize the poetry of this simple act. Our magic hour has drawn to a close. I light the lamp, fold up the day, and unfurl the night.

DREAMER

"You seem to have a special rapport with Dreamer," the trainer tells me. "We'll put you in the lagoon with her tomorrow."

That night, I can barely sleep. I keep picturing Dreamer, her head rising above the water, looking quizzically at me.

It is with some embarrassment that I remember my wish/prayer, two years earlier, in front of the icon Panagia Myrtidiotissa (mer-tro-dye-tiss-ah), the Madonna of the Myrtle Tree, sequestered within the flagstone courtyard of the Palianis monastery in Crete. A group tour had taken me to the centuries-old Greek monastery where several nuns, barely younger than a century, sat, draped in black, crocheting lace beneath trellises covered in bougainvillea boughs and clusters of plump green grapes.

The nuns relayed the story of their miraculous icon through a translator. One nun pointed her arthritic finger toward an ancient, sprawling myrtle tree, its limbs reminding me of a thousand-armed bodhisattva. Fascinated, I watched a group of women gather hand in hand around the tree, singing softly. People from around the world had affixed ribbons, rosaries, and prayers that dangled from different boughs of the tree. I had been told of this custom before leaving home and had packed an offering of my own: a small fragment of a tree limb, no bigger than my little finger.

My offering, tied with a purple ribbon, belonged to my favorite tree, an oak heavy with twisted moss, which had offered midday shade to my grandpa's cows and a childhood hiding place for me. I loved that tree like a mother, and, like a mother, the oak welcomed me, time and again, into her outspread arms and soothed my spirit with hushed whispers of wind that slid in and around me.

Years later, when I visited the oak one last time, I thanked her for the sustenance of her deep roots during my nomadic childhood. As a keepsake, I bent to pick up a slender branch from the ground beneath her aging canopy. I wanted some piece of her to take home and hold from time to time. The hours I spent straddling her branches, pressing my back against her trunk, and sensing her rising sap taught me everything I needed to know about place, rootedness, and belonging.

What better offering to a holy, ancient tree in Greece than a piece of my mother tree? Evidently, the Madonna of the Myrtle Tree shared a very special relationship with a tree as well.

"The icon of the Madonna," the translator said, nodding toward the tree, "was discovered there near the myrtle's roots."

The icon, enshrined in a silver and glass case, had been built into the wall surrounding the tree. Purportedly, the nuns who first found the icon removed it from the tree and carried it inside the chapel to protect it. The very next morning, however, the icon had mysteriously reappeared in the tree. Each time the nuns carried the icon inside, they woke to find it back in the tree. Finally, the nuns acquiesced and allowed the icon to remain outside in nature.

It was at this point in the story that the nun cautioned, "If you say a prayer to the Panagia Myrtidiotissa and your prayers are granted, you must return here to thank her."

I inwardly smiled; I did plan to ask for something, but I could not imagine returning to this obscure old monastery, six thousand miles away from my writing desk, even if my wish were granted. First, I knotted the purple ribbon holding the slender piece of wood from my oak onto the myrtle tree, and then I edged closer to the icon of the Madonna to make a simple wish.

I call it a wish instead of a prayer because my request lacked both altruism and grandeur. Though I was earnest, I could have prayed for so many other causes, or for so many deserving people, which is why I blush, remembering. Instead, the desire at the center of my heart, at that moment, was simply to swim with a dolphin.

My friend Sue, on that same trip, laughed good-naturedly when I poked fun at my wish. I told her I had basically asked to swim with a *fish*, even though I know dolphins are not fish. Had I squandered an opportunity to wish for something more meaningful, with more gravitas? In my defense, I had just finished a semester in graduate school researching the symbolism of dolphins for a world mythologies class.

Greeks, with their two-thousand-plus islands, regarded dolphins very highly. Dolphins adorn numerous ancient

Greek vases, Minoan dolphin frescoes decorate the palace of Knossos, and Poseidon himself placed a constellation in the sky, honoring the dolphin Delphinus (which is why it was so serendipitous and meaningful to learn that the star Sue and I named belonged to this very constellation). The Greeks decreed the dolphin their national animal, and killing one, in ancient times, was punishable by death.[39] Countless stories of dolphins coming to the aid of people at sea explain their status as super creatures, messengers, protectors, and angels of the sea.

Perhaps my wish, uttered on Greek soil, held more gravitas than I imagined.

Years later, a chain of events has led me to a pod of bottlenose dolphins here in Florida, to a reputable place that humanely offers therapeutic dolphin swims to people with illnesses and disabilities. I feel fortunate to be here, especially since I am both well and able-bodied. I have listened to the trainers, taken the tour, and learned about dolphin etiquette—things I should do, like keep my hands next to my body, and things I shouldn't do, like attempt to hang on.

After tussling with my snorkel and fins, I slip into the tepid lagoon of salt water and sink below the surface. In a world of opaque blue, I hear door-hinge creaks, trills, and high-pitched whistles, even before I see the arcs of their bodies. The precision of a dolphin's echolocation can determine the difference between a golf ball and a ping-pong ball based solely on density. I feel like I am being ultrasonically scanned, like the dolphins are *reading* me.

If so, they know how eager I am to interact. Within minutes, two dolphins glide swiftly and silently past me, seemingly uninterested, pricking my expectation. The dolphins circumnavigate another woman and linger at her side. I look from side to side and wait, expectantly, one ticking minute after another. Still nothing. I feel like a wallflower at the sock hop, waiting to be asked to dance. Then, I scold myself, *When have you ever been this close to a dolphin? Be in the present moment. Watch them interacting with others!*

I let go of my grasping desire to interact and content myself with watching. How can these air-breathing creatures be so elegant and one with the water? Their movements look like a water ballet. I truly am mesmerized to be this close.

All of a sudden, I feel a pressure against the back of my knee and, whoosh, I'm being carried forward at an amazing speed. I had not seen the dolphin approach from behind. Unbelievably, I'm somehow riding a dolphin all the way back to the dock. The sensation thrills me and causes my heart to pound in my chest.

But the trainer . . . she will think I'm holding on.

I sputter to the surface, yank out my snorkel, and shake my head. "I didn't do anything. I wasn't holding on."

She nods. "I know. That's Dreamer. Evidently, she wants to play with you."

I dive back underwater, kick my fins, and swim away from the dock again. Dreamer appears and gives me another ride back. Despite my snorkel, I smile and giggle, swallowing a gulp of salt water. Again, I swim toward the center of the lagoon. This time Dreamer swims beneath me and rolls her white belly toward mine. Not more than two feet separate us. I meet her eye, such a gentle, piercing gaze, so seemingly wise.

I think back to that afternoon at the monastery when

I offered a piece of my mother tree to the myrtle tree and asked a serene-faced Madonna for this very experience. I no longer harbor any embarrassment or a need to minimize my wish. I just glide alongside Dreamer, absorbing the bliss and mystery of peering into her eyes.

Trust what is deep, in the center of your heart, I would tell my younger self. Don't be afraid to pray or wish for it, no matter how simple or naive it may seem. Don't make light of your longings. There are holy places in that deep center of yours, icons of communion and utter bliss. Don't dismiss or be embarrassed by them; honor them. They will change you for the better. You have an affinity for the earth and the sea. Let yourself delve there, without apology.

And one more thing. Should you ever make a wish to the Panagia Myrtidiotissa in a small monastery in Crete, know that you will indeed *return there, years later, to say thank you.*

I go to bed that night, reliving my dolphin swim over and over in my mind. My body still tingles beneath the sheets, and warmth spreads over me like a blanket. Joy—that's what I feel pulsing through me. Dreamer gave this wallflower the dance of her life.

PAUL'S BEACH RENTALS

He jabs a long drill bit into the sand, drilling multiple holes, evenly spaced, for the poles of dozens of green and yellow umbrellas. After threading the umbrellas into their appropriate slots, he unloads sugar-white chaise lounges from a trailer that's hooked behind his golf cart; his strength makes the lounges appear lighter than they actually are. Finally, for the pièce de résistance, he plops canary-yellow cushions on top of the chaises, providing extra comfort for his seaside customers.

By my calculations, Paul has set up and taken down his umbrellas and chairs more than twenty thousand times—twice a day for more than thirty years.

I'm not sure when, exactly, we began to recognize each other. Mandy barely reached my waist, and Paul had not yet kissed a bride. In fact, the chairs and umbrellas Paul set up at that time did not belong to him. He worked as an employee. His smile struck me, even then, along with his finger wave, whenever I passed the beach hut during my walks. I noticed that he recognized others, too. Numerous people stopped to chat.

Anytime you ask Paul how he's doing, he will likely respond, "I couldn't be better." And then, motioning toward the Gulf, he might add, "Look at this view." I have heard him say, "I'm the luckiest man alive," "I have the best job in world," and "I wouldn't trade this for anything." Paul's positive attitude and his delight in what he does are gifts to those of us who tread these sands. Other beach stands dot the dunes up and down this strand of beach, but no one has impacted me like Paul, and I am a passerby, not even a customer.

The sum of our brief conversations over the years provides a snapshot of Paul. He and his brother married sisters, and both couples had twins. Paul eventually bought out the beach stand from his employer. A third child completed his family, and then, amazingly, we talked about his twins heading off for college. Once, our chat turned more serious. Paul told me he was having medical issues.

"I'll say prayers for you," I told him. And I did. And, I suspect, a lot of other beach goers did as well. (Thankfully, all turned out well.)

So impactful are these seemingly brief encounters that I remember, still, another man, more than forty-five years ago, in upstate New York. He was like Paul. Jim and I owned only one car back then, so I drove Jim to work. Every morning, we passed a traffic cop waving his arms, like a conductor guiding a symphony of cars. Even on the coldest, blustery days, the traffic cop's toothy smile reached through the windshield and warmed me like summer sunshine. I waved to him sometimes. I can still picture him standing there. I wish he knew, somehow, the lasting fragrance of his memory. Just once, I wish I had rolled down my window to shout, *Thank you for the way you brighten my day.*

Not wanting history to repeat itself, I decide to tell Paul I'm writing a piece about our years of hellos. I want to tell him that his simple, steady, and positive presence on the beach has been a gift to me. I want to tell him how beautifully he exemplifies *loving what you do and being where you are.*

One of the brightest lights, I would tell my younger self, is the light of our genuine self, shining through our circumstances. Ponder this. What would it take for you to say, "I am the happiest woman alive. I would not trade my life for anything"?

Put love into your doing. No apologies, no judgments. Let joy find you, wherever you are, arranging colorful rows of umbrellas on a white-sand beach, or standing at an intersection on a cold, blustery day. If you love where you are and what you are doing, you may have twenty thousand opportunities to feel good about it, twenty thousand opportunities to shine your light on another life, twenty thousand opportunities to teach contentment.

On the receiving side, when you are moved by someone's random act of kindness, a warm smile, or a joyful hello, roll down the imaginary window between the two of you, meet his or her gaze and say thank you—be it with words, a note, or a nod. Do it in the moment, while you can.

Don't wait forty years.

I print out my story and carry it toward Paul on the beach. My shyness begs me to turn around, but I keep walking. I see him then, ahead, bending over his crossword puzzle. A smile spreads across his face when he sees me. I catch my reflection in his sunglasses.

"I wrote something . . . about you," I say, handing him my pages. "I guess you could say it's like a thank-you note. For being the person you are."

He takes my pages, my offering, this modest man who loves his life by the sea, and he begins to read. I cannot be sure, since Paul's face is whiskered and tanned, but I think I see a flush of pink creep across his cheeks. I have no doubt about his broad, infectious smile.

OLIVIA & OLIVER

I froze, midstep, the first time I saw the osprey. I crouched on the bedroom floor, drew up my knees, and watched her through the screen, spellbound, for the better part of an hour, afraid even to scratch my itchy nose for fear I would frighten her away. I did not know that she planned to visit regularly, or that, in a manner of speaking, she planned to be my new neighbor.

I spontaneously named her Olivia, my genus name for all female ospreys. Only later did I discover Olivia means olive branch, although Olivia hardly resembles the dove-like harbinger of peace. Her wingspan covers more than five feet. She is a magnificent wild osprey with powerful thighs, a white crest atop her head, dark feather sideburns, and piercing yellow eyes, equipped with a third eyelid. This eyelid functions like a goggle, allowing her to see underwater when she dives for fish. Her diving and hunting prowess give rise to other nomenclature for her species: sea hawks, fish hawks, and sea eagles.

This afternoon, Olivia teeters drunkenly on my balcony

railing. Her razor-sharp talons click against the metal rails as she tries to balance a newly caught fish, held in a death grip. Satisfied, she stabs her short, hooked beak into the fish. I grimace, knowing full well the mess that is about to ensue. Unlike a pelican, swallowing its fish whole, Olivia tears her raw fish into bite-size pieces, flicking scales and blood about. And for some reason, not yet clear to me, she eats almost everything except fish eyeballs. More than once, after she flies away, I have collected the disembodied eyeballs and tossed them into a garbage bag.

Admittedly, the eyeballs disgust me. Ospreys can be so messy, both with eating fish and projectile pooping, that many of my neighbors have strung up fishing line and sharp points on their balcony rails to keep the ospreys away. I cannot bring myself to do this. Olivia needs a safe zone, I reason. Plus, observing a wild bird at such a close proximity fascinates me. Many a guest has oohed and awed, watching her antics through the window: the way she zigzags her head when she sees something, the way she cheeps at other ospreys flying nearby, and the way she can turn her head, owl-like, almost 160 degrees.

The good outweighs the bad, although Jim does not agree. He would prefer to shoo her off our tidy balcony. So we made a deal. If he promises not to scare her away, I will clean up her mess. This has been our arrangement for the various ospreys who have visited us for close to two decades—one of the many compromises we have made during our fifty-plus years together. Like the ospreys, Jim and I chose to mate for life, returning again and again to our long-ago wedding vows.

I must admit, however, that I sometimes envy Jim's end

of this particular bargain—especially when I lug out my Olivia cleaning kit, a bucket filled with disposable rubber gloves, trash bags, paper towels, a spray bottle filled with disinfectant, brushes, and a foam knee pad. I try to convince myself that cleaning up the muck is a form of exercise.

Although I haven't mentioned him, Olivia has a mate, Oliver. A derivative of Olivia, and my genus for all male ospreys, Oliver is smaller and a tad slighter than Olivia. Ospreys mate for life. Programmed with an internal calendar, Olivia and Oliver begin nesting in December, reusing the same nest every year, masterfully constructed on a channel marker within sight of our condo. Their nest, made of branches and twigs on the outside and lined with softer grasses and seaweed on the inside, withstands gale-force winds that sometimes topple our plants and porch furniture. I cannot fathom how two handless birds manage to wedge large branches and twigs into something so huge, solid, and durable.

They face construction mishaps, to be sure. I have seen them swoop down onto the beach, grasp a piece of driftwood between their talons, and fly off toward the channel marker. Through my binoculars, I have also seen that very piece of wood accidentally splash into the water as they try to secure it into place. But they persevere, over and over, until finally completing their tedious and arduous task of rebuilding their nest. Within six weeks, their efforts will be rewarded with fuzzy fledglings.

When you set your mind to building a dream, persevere, I would tell my younger self. Try again and again, no matter how tedious and arduous the task. Effort, determination, and commitment are well spent on endeavors that put you in touch with wild, messy, untamed possibility.

And when making choices, do not necessarily choose that which is easiest; choose rather that which is most enduring, that which can help feather potential.

Build something strong on the outside and soft on the inside. This is especially true in marriage; build a beautiful nest of give-and-take, a safe nest to raise children, an enduring nest to weather life's storms, and a softly lined nest to fledge gentle togetherness.

Olivia, full-bellied and content, has spent the better part of the afternoon on the balcony, staring out to sea—something I enjoy as well. She knows nothing of a woman with a cleaning kit, admiring her from afar.

It is a bargain worth keeping.

THE PILGRIM SHELL

The surf coughs up a scallop shell, colored and shaped like a sunrise. I scurry to pick it up before the waves reclaim it. Water drips down my wrist as I rub the rough, ribbed lines between my fingertips. Something pricks my thumb, which I reflexively soothe in my mouth, tasting the saltiness of the sea. My skin is not broken, but, upon further examination, I see that the shell is. That won't do. I lob it back into the surf. I want near-perfect specimens, eighteen to twenty of them.

I'm more than a beachcomber this morning—more like a wayfarer, on a mission to collect scallop shells for my friend Trisha. I agreed, since I live on the beach, to bring her some when I join her in a few short weeks, for the tour she's leading. A dozen and a half other women from the United States will be joining me, as we journey together, under Trisha's competent and watchful eye, throughout Spain. Scallop shells represent pilgrimage, and Trisha wants to present every woman with one upon our arrival in Barcelona.

Pausing by a mound of shells above the tideline, I poke the toe of my sneaker into the mound. Grains of sand flick against my ankle and into my sock as a waterfall of shells clacks and cascades around my foot. Two perfectly intact scallop shells rest on top of the heap: one a deep burgundy with speckles of white fanning out from its center, and the other a pale, pale pink. I never tire of the scallops' palette of colors, as unique as ten thousand sunsets. Genes alone cannot claim credit for the different hues and blushes. Diet and the water environment also influence the varied colorations, which may explain why I find more abundant numbers of one color versus another in different years.

The fan shape of the scallop shell also pleases me, its loveliness worthy of bearing up Renaissance painter Botticelli's copper-haired Venus in *The Birth of Venus*. She stands within the shell, one heel resting on the smooth curve where the shell's grooves merge. Maybe the very structure of the scallop shell speaks to pilgrimage—the many diverse lines and paths culminating in one central place, the crux where Venus stands. And what better vessel for birthing beauty than the fanned, fluted edges of the scallop, mirrored by architects worldwide?

The fluted edges of the last two scallop shells I just retrieved from the shell mound pass inspection; I clink their perfectly symmetrical shapes into my bag and peer inside. Trisha should be pleased.

In fact, Trisha, whose hair reminds me of the copper locks of Botticelli's Venus, is very pleased when I hand her my bag of shells, weeks later. Still a bit jet-lagged, I watch as Trisha places into our palms, one by one, a shell symbolic of our upcoming journey. She tucks a copper-colored shell into mine. I smile, wondering if she somehow knows that copper-colored scallops are my favorite, or if a synchronicity has just tapped me on the shoulder. Either way, I feel excitement and anticipation for the days ahead.

One of the trip's highlights, for me, will be walking a small portion of the famous Camino de Santiago trail. Although we will walk only a few miles of the trail, our footsteps will overlay the footsteps of millions of pilgrims who, for more than a thousand years, have walked the entire five-hundred-mile journey from France through Spain to the crux, the final resting place of St. James. Camino de Santiago means *The Way of St. James.*

I have nothing against St. James; in fact, I find his admonition—"everyone should be quick to listen, slow to speak, and slow to become angry"[40]—good advice. But at the core of me, I most connect with the pre-Christian lore that this ancient trail Via Finisterre[41] follows the path of the Milky Way, an earthly path of stars, all the way to land's end, the end of the world at the edge of the sea in Galicia, where scallop shells adorn the shore. I know of no other place on earth said to follow the path of the Milky Way.

Several days into our trip, the opportunity to walk the earthly path of stars has arrived. Our bus lurches to a stop on one of the narrow village streets of Cirueña, in the province of La Rioja. Descending from the bus, my legs welcome the opportunity to stretch and walk on the brick sidewalk. Cool air lifts the edge of my jacket and carries the aroma of mouthwatering paella simmering nearby. Up ahead, I spot the likeness of a scallop shell embedded into the cornerstone of a building. We pass numerous royal-blue signs with bright-yellow arrows pointing the way to the Camino de Santiago. Stylized yellow scallop shells accompany the arrows. Scallops appear everywhere—painted on a wooden barrel, hanging in shop windows, inlaid in a mosaic.

Scallop shells, we learned, are the most iconic and well-known symbol of the Camino de Santiago; early pilgrims often gathered them from the sea and brought them home as proof they had completed their arduous journey. Our journey, however, will not be so arduous. We are day-trippers, walking only the afternoon from the village of Cirueña to our hotel in Santo Domingo de la Calzada, a few miles away. I finger the scallop shell in my pocket and look for the emblazoned blue signs that guide us to the outskirts of the village.

Pavement dissolves into an unpaved path; village noises dissolve into birdsong, and the scent of paella bows to the cologne of the earth and her fields. The Camino ribbons toward a knoll, the distant hills beyond, and, farther still, toward blue mountains softened by the afternoon haze. The scene resembles a watercolor painting—muted sky, differing shades of brown fields to either side, dotted by brushstrokes of dark green along the ocher-colored road. I imagine this road at night, illumined by a million stars cascading across the sky in the veil of the Milky Way.

Trisha forges ahead, her long legs taking determined strides that crunch on loose pebbles as the distance grows between us. Her hair billows in the breeze, and her trench coat flutters behind her; she is a vision of confidence, determination, and comfort. We lovingly call her *tour mother*. I am grateful to be on this trip, so much so that I want to run up and give her a hug. But I stop myself. I want this walk to be mindful—both for her and for me. We are, after all, walking the sacred path of earthly stars.

With that in mind, I take a deep breath and sink into the present moment. I am here, right here, where my feet touch the earth, feeling the air against my cheeks, listening to the call of an unknown bird. I walk, thinking little. I'm too far away from home to worry about dinner, schedules, and countless lists of things to be crossed off. My only task today, at this very moment, is to attend to my steps, one after the other. Five words take on the rhythm of my foot-steps. Life . . . is . . . such . . . a . . . gift. Life . . . is . . . such . . . a . . . gift. The words become like a mantra and my footsteps the metronome. Life . . . is . . . such . . . a . . . gift.

I've sometimes squandered this gift—especially in my younger years—mostly through impatience. In my hurry to reach a milestone, meet a deadline, or get through a day, I rarely noted the bigger picture: we are spiritual beings walking a human path beneath the stars. What's the rush? Why not savor the journey? My tightly wound, hurry-up pace has found fewer footholds in my life these days. Tapping my feet, strumming the steering wheel, and eyeing the clock have morphed into things like watching waves, admiring a sunset, and pocketing a shell.

I hear again the unknown bird call and continue my walk in solitude until I pass a woman, tanned by the sun and wearing a faded blue and red bandanna. She sits on her haunches, sipping from a well-used water bottle, a heavy backpack askew by her side. She is no day-tripper. Still, she smiles. Neither of us speaks, yet I feel a palpable unspoken communication between us, a gossamer thread of shared experience. No matter where we come from, who we are, or how we vote, we are, at that very moment, both pilgrims traveling the same path.

I notice she wears a scallop shell pendent. I slip my fingers inside my pocket and pull out my copper-colored shell for her to see. She nods. This is all that needs to be said.

All of us are pilgrims, I would tell my younger self, journeying through the Milky Way toward an unfamiliar destination. Our many paths, like the fanned lines of the scallop shell, guide us to a central point, the crux, where one journey ends, marked by the last breath we draw, and another unknown journey begins. In this life, our outside shell is differently colored by our environment and life experiences. But, at our core, most all of us fellow pilgrims want the same things: to be safe, to be loved and valued, and to be relevant. Life is not so much about the destination; it is more about appreciating the journey, valuing the people we meet along the way, and remembering, with each step we take: life . . . is . . . such . . . a . . . gift!

Back home, on my island, my copper-colored pilgrim shell lies among my collection of shells. Its lines and fluted edges bear a quiet testimonial to the watercolor landscape of Spain; to my dear, openhearted friend Trisha, her copper-colored hair blowing in the breeze; and to the crunch of footsteps along the path of the Milky Way.

MANY LAMPS, ONE LIGHT

"What do you want for Mother's Day?" Mandy asks, her voice as cheery as the sun splashing across my living-room shelves. She has called to ask because I am, admittedly, somewhat hard to buy for, especially since we downsized to our condominium. I don't have a lot of patience for clutter. Trying to create positive feng shui, I cleared out most of my baubles and trinkets. *No more tchotchkes for me*, I heard myself say. Although I must confess, a number of valued exceptions still pepper my office shelves.

In my younger years, I focused more on acquisitions: like the one in front of me, my prized watermelon-size bailer shell, occupying much of the top living-room shelf. Sailors of old used these wide-mouthed, cream-colored shells to bail water from the bottom of their boats. I came upon the shell in an old shop, heard the story, and was smitten with its history. The idea of possessing such a lovely, useful shell took me back to my days of imagining the deserted island of my youth.

To be sure, I still value my bailer shell and its purchase, but these days I'm more inclined toward divesting. I have been asking for gifts that need no dusting and leave only footprints, so to speak, like restaurant gift certificates, an audiobook, or, one of my very favorite gifts, a voucher to ride on the *Dolphin Explorer*, where I never fail to see a dolphin.

I surprise myself, then, by telling Mandy that I would like a collector's edition of six leather-bound books to sit on the adjoining shelf in the living room, on the opposite side of the bailer shell. The unexpected nature of my request surprises not only me but Mandy as well.

"Really," she says, her tone more of a question mark than an exclamation point.

She doesn't yet realize the significance that these books hold for me, or even how the idea came to me some months before.

Earlier that fall, my poet-textile-artist friend Curly, whose poems stitch words together as exquisitely as her hands turn cloth and thread into stories and wings, asked the girlfriends, on our girlfriend vacation, to join her for a visit to Houston's Rothko Chapel. Rothko was, she said, one of her favorite artists.

We answered *of course*; it was *her* day, after all.

One hour later, we parked in front of the brick chapel, founded by philanthropists John and Dominique de Menil. Over one hundred thousand people a year, from different faiths the world over, visit the intimate chapel. Its mission is *to inspire people to action through art and contemplation, to nurture reverence for the highest aspirations of humanity, and to provide a forum to explore matters of worldwide concern.*

Upon entering, I hushed into silence, taken with the meditative environment and the enormous canvases of Mark Rothko. Each was nuanced and unique, even though all fourteen paintings were painted black—light black, dark black, striated black. I never realized black had so many hues. The canvases reminded me of the great void of night that has yet given birth to light. It occurred to me, in that cloistered room, that each visitor was the light, hundreds of thousands of human candles lighting up that space every year.

What struck me, too, were the wisdom books scattered along the benches as I entered the sanctuary. I read the covers: the Bible, Koran, Torah, Tao Te Ching, Bhagavad Gita, and others. Surely, people of all faiths felt welcome in this space, their sacred text shining light into the darkness. I thought of Rumi's quote "The lamps are different, But the Light is the same."[42]

As I scanned the canvases hugging the chapel walls and the visitors whispering before them, the truth of Rumi's words vibrated deeply in my core. Each holy book, and the faith it signified, represented a different lamp, shining into the darkness with its own unique particularity, but the light and the wisdom of which it spoke, its fire, stemmed from one source. How easy, but nearsighted, to focus on the differences between the lamps instead of recognizing the one radiant light emanating from them all.

"So," I finish telling Mandy on the phone, "what I would love for Mother's Day is a small collection of wisdom books to grace my shelves, as a reminder that there are many lamps but only one light."

"Done," she said.

People are not as different as you might imagine, I would tell my younger self. It is noble to seek and find wisdom in the places that speak most loudly to your heart. But remember, your lamp is not the only lamp shining in the darkness. There are other lamps of different sizes, hues, and colors. We cannot know the entirety of infinity; none of us has a corner on truth no matter our lamp. Even something as seemingly simple and obvious as the color black has many nuances and hues. Your task, then, is not to insist that everyone's lamp should look the same as yours; no, your task is simply to raise the lamp you choose, and become a channel through which the universal light of love can shine.

And consider this. A simple act, seemingly for someone else, like saying yes to a friend who would like your company, can take you to unexpected places you might never travel to on your own. Gifts lie buried in unexpected places—especially places frequented by poets and artists, who have a keen eye for lamplight.

Not long after our phone conversation, Mandy sent me the collector's edition. Bound in blue leather and gilded in gold: the Gospels, the Koran, the Dhammapada, the Bhagavad Gita, the Torah, and the Tao Te Ching grace my living-room shelves. I have read parts of all of them, and each contain pearls of wisdom. Sometimes I reverently drag my fingertip across their embossed gold names.

They are one of my favorite Mother's Day gifts—my prized collection of sacred lamps.

CONCH THROWER

As a rule, the year offers only twelve of these mornings, with an occasional thirteenth thrown in every so often. The full opal moon bows in the west at the same moment the sun peeks above the horizon in the east. To witness the juxtaposition of these two luminaries, visible on opposite horizons at the same moment, ranks as one of my rare pleasures, which is why I am particularly dismayed by what I see lying up ahead.

Littering a long strand of beach, I eye hundreds and hundreds of stranded Florida fighting conchs; their spired, conical shells look like gleaming jewels flung in a rage against the sand. On the one hand, I feel like hugging nature's neck for the morning extravaganza on the horizons, but, on the other, I feel like scolding her for her extravagant waste and disregard for the sea creatures struggling before me.

The gulls, squawking and flapping overhead, do not share my chagrin. From their point of view, it's a lucky day. They draw circles in the sky, coming back for second and third helpings of the banquet laid before them, their extended stomachs heavy with tasty conch flesh.

The conchs' life-or-death struggle to survive eclipses the morning's celestial significance. Haplessly tossed toward shore by rough seas and shipwrecked on the beach, some of them jerk and stab their foot, trying to tumble themselves back into the sea. Some have already lost the survival-of-the-fittest battle, their bodies oozing from their shells, looking like parched tongues splayed upon the sand. In time, the sun, sea, and birds will clean out the flesh of the dying conchs, leaving an unusual number of pristine shells on the shore for the next few days.

Collectors covet the conch's four- to five-inch shell, with its polished mahogany interior spiraling mysteriously inward. I love to place my ear on the spiraled opening and listen to the whisper of the sea within. Many vacationers do not know the difference between a live or dead shell until their hotel room, or worse, their suitcase, fills with a nose-wrinkling stench. Taking live shells can be smelly, and, in our county, it's also illegal.

Univalves, like the conch, pose the greatest threat of being collected live because, from the outside, their exterior looks the same; the live animal retracts deep into the shell. Unlike conchs, bivalves, such as scallops, are obviously dead. When a bivalve dies, the shell opens, the flesh falls out, and the two halves of the shell separate in the surf. If both halves of a bivalve cling snugly together, like a lady's compact, the shell is alive.

The best indicator of a live conch is the hard, claw-like trapdoor, the operculum, which protects the animal inside the shell. I often see these hard opercula washed up on the beach after the conch dies. Most go unnoticed, easily mistaken for a piece of bark or other debris. But if the operculum is firmly attached to the shell, the conch is alive.

Eyeing the field of struggling conchs before me, I imagine there also will be a profusion of opercula washing ashore in the next few weeks. It is at this moment that I see a mother and her pigtailed daughter bending and picking up conchs and gently dropping them into the folds of the mother's outstretched skirt.

I wonder if the mother knows about the law against taking live shells. Does she even know that some of the shells in her skirt are likely alive? I seesaw about whether to say something. But my dilemma quickly dissolves as I watch the mother and daughter walk toward the breaking waves and begin to toss the conchs from the mother's skirt, one by one, into the life-giving water.

The sight of them reels me back to a day, years earlier, when Mandy, about the same age as the pigtailed girl in front of me, plucked up conch after conch, throwing them back into the sea. Moved, back then, by Mandy's innocence, her open heart, and her earnest effort, I joined her. I targeted the especially tenacious conchs, the ones that struggled to move themselves toward the water in what, I later learned, is called a *strombid leap*: when the conch digs its operculum into the sand and uses it to hop forward, much like a mini pole vaulter.

Mandy and I had been inspired by the conchs trying to push and roll themselves toward the waves, but eventually, after dozens of tosses, maybe even hundreds, with sweat dripping across our brows, we had to surrender our pursuit. The tightened muscles in my back refused to assist any more bends toward the shore.

"We can't save them all," I told Mandy.

Reluctantly, she followed me home.

The mother and pigtailed girl will likely come to the same conclusion.

But . . .

Should the fact that not all conchs can be saved mean that we should never toss a struggling one into the water? I think not. I believe something strengthens inside the heart of conch throwers, be it compassion, a belief that every act of kindness matters, or the gratification of helping something as small and seemingly inconsequential as one conch among a thousand. Nature may have no need of this intervention, but the soul may.

What will be required of you as you grow older, I would tell my younger self, is expanding your ability to hold the paradoxes of life without becoming apathetic, overwhelmed, or cynical. Life is, by its very nature, paradoxical. The inhale juxtaposes the exhale; ebb tide juxtaposes flood tide; the waxing moon juxtaposes the waning moon; birth juxtaposes death; one act of tossing conchs into the sea juxtaposes leaving a thousand others to die. Waving hello most often requires waving goodbye. What can we do in the face of these never-ending cycles, woven into the fabric of life, but grow large enough to hold the confusion of a finite mind, trying to feel its way through the fog of paradox.

Think of your dreams filled with life-affirming images: flying horses, friends, helpers, idyllic scenes and scenarios so powerful you feel uplifted when awakened. Juxtaposed against these dreams are the frustrating dreams of never arriving, forgetting something important, being chased, or worse, encountering an image so frightening you awaken, flooded with relief it was only a nightmare. Life, I think, is similar to a dream. What if, when we die, we actually awaken to discover that everything we have experienced is not, in the most literal sense, real—not the total sum of existence? What if the words of the nursery rhyme "Row, Row, Row Your Boat"[43] *are true? What if life really is "but a dream"? What matters, then, is not so much what happens to us but how we respond to what happens to us, or, put more melodically, how gently we row our boat down the stream.*

Take the conch throwers, for instance. While they cannot save all the conchs, they can hold the joy of knowing they cared enough to gather a few of them into their skirts and toss them back into a life-giving sea.

One person cannot help everyone, but if everyone helped one person, what a different world this would be.

Eventually, I turn away from the mother and daughter, who are still rescuing conchs. On my walk back to the condo, my eyes notice a shell; it jerks and rolls. My back complains only mildly as I bend, pick up the conch, its operculum snapping shut, and lob it as far as I can beyond the waves.

THE DEEP

The brim of my sun hat skims the salt water, giving off the odor of fresh straw, a smell I well remember from my younger, horseback-riding days in West Texas. Bicycling my feet and circling my arms, I tread water, riding the gentle swells—a perfect outdoor exercise—this cloudless August morning.

Water splashes my face, and a droplet runs down the right lens of my sunglasses as I bob to and fro in the current. I am keeping an eye about me for what swims below the water's surface; this week I spotted a small sand shark, snooping around the rock point to my right. Though shark attacks are extremely rare—since 1882, there have been only seven attacks in our surrounding area[44]—I am vigilant.

Warm summer waters attract more marine life. Black clouds of fish, schools numbering in the tens of thousands, coalesce in kaleidoscope fashion beneath the surface. This week, a baby dolphin scattered the schools as it tried to synchronize its surfacing and descent into the water with its mother.

Then, just yesterday, a large manatee, satisfying its curiosity, glided silently past me, so close I saw its thick skin marred by a sickle-shaped white scar along its side. Most adult manatee bear scars; their slow, lolling movements make them vulnerable to boat propellers. Even though the manatee neared ten feet long, and undoubtedly weighed close to a ton, it did not frighten me. Manatees pose no danger. Florida's state marine mammal is a gentle giant, a curious aquatic relative of the elephant.

The aquatic world, covering seventy-one percent of the earth's surface and teeming with marine life, fascinates me, which may explain my relative ease in the water and my flirtations with scuba diving over the years. I'm not certified, but I have gone on several diving expeditions with instructors.

I smile, remembering the last time I went. I signed Mandy up to accompany me. The instructor told our group that we needed to pass the swimming-pool test. If that went well, he said, we could dive together in open water.

Mandy smiled and excitedly lifted her shoulders.

"Anyone here have experience?" the blond, tanned instructor asked.

I lifted my hand, giving Mandy a knowing look, probably one similar to Barney Fife when trying to impress Andy Taylor.

The instructor met my eyes and nodded. "Great, this will be review for you, then," he said, and he began explaining to the others how the regulator works; what to do if the regulator is accidentally kicked out of your mouth; and, most importantly, what to do if your mask accidentally fills up with water. "Very important to know how to clear your mask of water while underwater," he said.

Holding the top of his mask, which covered his eyes and nose, he demonstrated how to inhale a deep breath on the regulator and then exhale. "Exhale hard out your nose," he told us. "That's the only way to clear it of water."

Water inside a mask is not only irritating, it's dangerous. You would choke on the water if you accidentally inhaled through your nose.

So important was this task, the instructor showed us a second time, and laughingly added that people new to diving often do it wrong. Instead of vigorously exhaling air out their nose, they blow the air out through their mouth, which has no impact whatsoever.

I nodded my head and laughed robustly. I felt like the instructor and I were simpatico; I had gone over these basics a number of times. Still, I tried to be respectful of the beginners.

Eventually, we suited up in our masks, fins, tanks, and regulators for the pool test. We formed a circle underwater and the instructor faced us one by one, making sure we knew how to clear our mask. He pointed to Mandy. I felt nervous for her; this was her first time. She held her mask, inhaled, and then exhaled hard through her nose.

I clapped underwater. She aced the test. A chip off the old block, I thought.

I was next. I held my mask with my palm, inhaled, and exhaled sharply out my mouth. The instructor waggled his finger no. I startled. Oh, right. How silly of me. I did exactly the opposite of what I was supposed to do.

I nodded my head and raised my finger indicating I would do it right this time.

Holding my mask, I inhaled and blew. Unbelievably, I

did it wrong again. By this time, Mandy was doubled over laughing, which is not an easy task at the bottom of a pool with a regulator in your mouth.

Now I was worried. I might be excluded from the dive. I palmed my hands together in a prayer position, asking for one last chance. Taking pity on me, the instructor nodded.

Hold mask, inhale, and exhale through nose.

Finally, I did it! The instructor allowed me to go.

Once in the cool, open water, we submerged into a liquid world of color. Sunlight dappled orange coral, iridescent blue fish, and purple sea urchins. Exotic sponges, bulbous sea-weed, and things so unfamiliar I could not determine if they were plant or animal dotted the sandy bottom. The whole watery world swayed this way and that with the current.

Diving takes me to a meditative place. My mind focuses only on the moment at hand. I watched the bubbles from Mandy's regulator pirouette toward the surface. Her brown hair floated around her, like a mermaid. She must have felt me looking at her; she lifted up her thumb, her eyes bright inside her mask. She was a natural.

The only sound was the *swooh, phew* of my own heavy, rhythmic breathing, like Darth Vader. Swooh. Phew. Swooh. Phew. In actuality, Darth Vader's breathing was created by inserting a microphone into a scuba regulator.[45]

Suddenly, Mandy pointed her finger repeatedly, indicating something behind me.

Alarmed, I swung around. A shadow moved toward me. When it came into full view, I marveled to see a jewel of the sea. A magnificent green sea turtle glided in the water. The up-and-down motion of her paddle-like flippers reminded me of the outstretched wings of a mighty bird, flying slow-motion through the air. On land, weighted by gravity, a female turtle might plod toward the dunes to lay a clutch of eggs, but there, in the watery depths, she swam with the grace of a ballerina.

The only measure of time passing was my pressure gauge, indicating that my oxygen level was getting low. Not surprisingly, my mermaid of a daughter had more oxygen left in her tank; either she exerted less energy, had more buoyancy, or just breathed easier. Without a second thought, she still wanted to surface with me. She rose to the top, breathless. Not because her tank was low on oxygen but because of the wonder she had just witnessed.

Swim in the deep, I would encourage my younger self. There are worlds to discover beyond this one. Some, below us, teem with aquatic life almost beyond the imagination. Such magic resides beneath the sea. Seventy-one percent of the world lies, for the most part, beyond our sight and outside our experience. How much more lies outside our awareness? Don't be afraid to find out.

Take a deep breath. Plunge in. Laugh at your shortcomings. Do the best you can. Don't shy away. Dive deep inside yourself, too, to places teeming with dreams, hopes, and memories, even if some are painful. In addition to scars, you will discover jewels. Transform that which is lumbering and awkward into something altogether new in the deep—unencumbered and completely free.

Get your feet wet. Risk wonder.

I adjust my straw hat with prune-wrinkled fingers, fondly remembering that scuba diving day with Mandy. A seagull dips near me, plucks up a shimmering, finger-size fish, and swallows it whole. The gull displays no fear of me, acting as if I belong to the sea.

I ask myself, *Am I a part of the sea? Or is the sea a part of me?*
Still treading water, I ponder this aquatic koan.
Slowly, an answer rises from the deep . . .
Yes!

ISLANDS IN THE MAKING

The sail clinks against the mast, and wind snaps it to attention. Our boat glides past the wild, knotted mangrove islands, knitted together by roots of the white, red, and black mangrove trees, part of the Ten Thousand Islands National Wildlife Refuge. As if on cue, several mangrove seeds, called propagules, float in the water not far from the hull. Each propagule holds within it the yet-to-be realized potential to create another island.

For a number of years, I propped a single propagule on my writing desk to remind me of the dormant, yet-to-be realized dream I had of writing a memoir. Quite frankly, the thought intimidated me; even years of effort could not guarantee my desired result. I didn't have an agent or an editor and was advised that I should write the book first. At times, I felt as alone as one of the mangrove propagules, bobbing aimlessly in a vast sea, with no assurance that my dream would find a place to alight.

The propagule on my desk gave me much-needed encouragement; it symbolized untapped potential and determination. I read memoir after memoir, which inspired me, but, on the flip side, also caused me to question if I was up to the task. So I also read books on the craft of writing and the art of telling stories. Sitting at my desk, day after day, month after month, I faithfully funneled my childhood onto paper. Word by word, inch by inch, I finally brought forth my book *Moonlight on Linoleum: A Daughter's Memoir.*

The crusty captain interrupts my train of thought.

"I seriously doubt that someone has counted these islands. There could be more than ten thousand." He grins, his unruly curls waving from beneath his sun-faded navy cap. His stubby finger points toward groves of waxy green canopies atop multiple-size islands, in various stages of creation, some as small as our local dinner-cruise ship and others large enough to inhabit.

I never tire of these forays into the uninhabited islands surrounding our island. I breathe in the sight of their untamed wildness, certain that even Darwin would be impressed by the evolution of this ecosystem. Not only are the mangrove forests exquisitely lush and green, growing at the edge of salt water, they are blue-carbon sponges when it comes to absorbing harmful carbon from the atmosphere, often storing three to five times more carbon than tropical forests.[46]

The meandering labyrinth of mangrove islands and narrow waterways of this thirty-five-thousand-acre estuary can be confusing. Paddlers and boaters, unfamiliar with the terrain, can easily lose their way. I have seen it happen. Once, a boat pulled alongside me and my kayak. The boater had rescued two lost women and their orange kayaks, which were thrown catawampus across the stern like two giant carrots. The women, sunburned and bedraggled, asked if I knew the location of the launch site where kayakers put in. I did know; the women were lost in my familiar corner of the estuary. I pointed out the cove, and off they went.

In defense of the lost kayakers, the islands and coves look much the same. I shade my eyes and look about. Mile upon mile, the tenacity of this mangrove forest stretches as far as my eyes can see. The refuge is part of the largest mangrove system in the Western Hemisphere, yet, ironically, each island owes its genesis to a green seedpod the length of a pencil.

These mangrove propagules bob, cork-like, in the water for several weeks until they absorb enough moisture to float upright and sprout roots. The hairy roots, like lost kayakers looking for a place to moor, grab onto oyster beds and sandbars. Eventually the roots trap sand, shells, and other debris, thereby adding another inch of real estate to the ever-expanding ten thousand islands.

The captain steers us toward a secluded mangrove island, perfect for beachcombing. He anchors just off a clump of rust-colored mangrove roots edging the water. I disembark barefoot into a foot of water and splash my way toward the sandy shore. I see a number of propagules washed up along the tide line. I pause. Why not prop another pod on my desk to symbolize my current writing project?

I released my other propagule after mailing off my *Moonlight* manuscript. I waded into the incoming tide and set the slender propagule afloat once again, grateful for its steady and silent encouragement as I wrote day after day. I released it with thanksgiving and imagined both the seed and my manuscript bobbing their way into the world in search of other shores.

Only now do I realize with some clarity that I have other islands-in-the-making, wanting and waiting to take root in the world.

Be patient, I would tell my younger self; island building takes time. Don't be deterred by the enormity of a dream or falter because it cannot be achieved immediately. There are ten thousand islands within you waiting to be born, but no need to fret. Allow them to evolve slowly, over time, inch by inch, day by day.

Let the daily tide of living fill in the spaces around the roots of your dreams with bits and pieces of what interests you, brings you joy, and fascinates you. Know that the dreams, bobbing around in your mind, have the ability to take root and grow.

If you should lose your way, reach out. Lean on the shoulders of another for a while. No shame there. Eventually, you will find your way back to yourself.

Measure progress in inches instead of miles, and, if necessary, prop an island-in-the-making on your desk.

A gust fills the sail and tips our boat leeward as we silently slice our way north, back to my island. I turn my face into the wind, grateful for all of the islands-in-the-making, the ones before me and the ones within me.

SUNKEN TREASURE

Mandy, known for her rings on many fingers, chose a flowered filigree ring in antique silver. It suited her perfectly. I, however, pored over the glass cases in the small jewelry store. Nothing spoke. Until I saw two lovely sterling silver bangles, each soldered with three antique etched beads.

Perfect, I thought.

That summer before college, both Mandy and I had felt a roller coaster of emotions: excitement, anticipation, fear, and sadness. To help ease our apprehension about living apart, I suggested we each buy a piece of jewelry to remind us of each other, something we could touch and wear.

Mandy and I are harmonious notes in the same chord. We finish each other's sentences and think of the most random story or fact at exactly the same moment, as if our brains fire with the very same neurons. But I majored in psychology. I know the importance of separation, individuation, and encouraging fledglings to fly. I also know that allowing us to feel closer and comforted by touching or wearing a piece of jewelry was well within the bounds of good mothering.

I picked up the first bangle from the glass case and slipped the cool silver circle onto my wrist. "This one represents you," I told Mandy, holding my arm up to the light. She leaned in to study the intricate pattern on the beads. The second circle jangled against the first as I slid it on. "And this one represents me. Know I will carry you with me always," I added.

Our brown eyes locked on each other, and we smiled.

I wear my bangles almost daily; their tinkling echoes the music of our many years together, up to college and, now, well beyond—from endless cuddles in the rocking chair to the joyful tears of graduations and marriage.

Most of my jewelry, like my bangles, has sentimental value—a story to tell, a milestone celebrated, or a passage marked.

So, today, as I fasten a silver pendant about my neck to walk down the beach for lunch, I am reminded of its story—one that began more than four hundred years ago. On September 6, 1622, the Spanish galleon *Nuestra Señora de Atocha* struck a coral reef and sank during a hurricane near the Florida Keys, just ninety miles south of where we live. Gold, copper, indigo, jewels, and two hundred thousand hand-stamped silver coins lay lost and buried at sea until the galleon was located in 1985.

The centerpiece of my pendant is one of the *Atocha*'s silver coins—four reales, hand-stamped with a Greek cross, minted in Potosi, Bolivia, and equivalent to one half of a sailor's monthly pay in the 1600s. My certificate of authenticity, complete with a raised seal, attests that my pendant is a true piece of sunken treasure.

However, I didn't purchase the necklace because I am a collector of sunken treasure.

Rather, I'm a collector of symbols and metaphors. My piece of sunken treasure represents an epiphany, of sorts, about the importance of reclaiming the lost and forgotten parts of ourselves: those silver coins within, minted with courage, confidence, and the belief that one voice matters. My piece of hand-stamped silver, intact after four hundred years buried in sand and salt water, speaks to the possibility of resurrecting and reclaiming shipwrecked treasure from our own unconscious, treasures that are ours for the taking.

I have worked to reclaim many qualities that were short-circuited in my growing-up years. Sadly, a fourth-grade teacher once made me sing a solo in front of the class about three ships sailing. Nervous, my alto voice warbled high and low, trying to locate the correct soprano notes. The ensuing laughter of my classmates caused hot tears to pool in my eyes. For years, I felt such shame and embarrassment about my voice. It wasn't until I rocked Mandy as a newborn that I reclaimed singing. Feeling Mandy's warmth against my breast, I opened my mouth and allowed the hesitant, healing notes of Brahms's Lullaby to fill the nursery.

Likewise, I had to reclaim my creativity. My mom often remarked that my sister was the creative one, and it wasn't until I had a dream about a mermaid bringing up treasures (a scene I later painted) that I began to reclaim my creativity. Self-worth, creativity, and a myriad of other qualities can become shipwrecked treasures relegated to the depths of the psyche.

Every time I fasten the clasp of this pendant about my neck, I think of its symbolism, and it emboldens me to reclaim the fullness of who I am. Someday, in what I hope will be the far distant future, my bangles and pendant will pass on to Mandy. She can wear and touch them in remembrance of me. I hope she, too, will feel emboldened. I hope she will hear the harmonious notes of our laughter in the tinkling of the bangles. I hope, when she fastens the clasp of the pendant about her neck, she, too, will remember to uncover the vast lode of treasures buried within her.

Reclaim the treasures that lie buried within you, I would encourage my younger self. Life, with its inevitable storms, can shipwreck aspects of yourself. What riches, minted in childhood, have been lost deep in the unconscious? Where is the confident, tinsel-haloed angel in the school Christmas play, waving to her grandma in the audience? Where is the young girl who fearlessly wrote her first novel in fourth grade? Where is the young woman who wanted to join the Peace Corps, believing she could make a difference in the world?

Confidence, perseverance, boldness, talent, optimism, belief—these are treasures worth salvaging. Never tire of your search to bring these minted pieces of yourself to the surface. Fashion them into centerpieces. Authenticate them as actual treasures from your deep. Wear them often. Turn them into heirlooms to be passed down to your daughter and all the daughters after her.

I walk down the beach toward lunch. My bangles jingle as I finger the pendant about my neck. Clouds skate across blue sky. I think about those three ships sailing, the *Nuestra Señora de Atocha*, and the gift of reclaimed treasure.

HOUSING CRISIS

Holding a tulip shell in my palm, I startle. The glossy, case-worthy shell, looking like a closed tulip bloom, moved. At least I think it did. I turn it over in my hand and catch a slight movement within the inward winding curve. It cannot be the mollusk itself, because its opercula, the trapdoor foot, is missing.

I hold very still. Seconds pass. Then two claws inch carefully out, then a pair of antennae, and finally two stalks, capped with round, electric-blue eyes. Upon seeing me, the creature startles and immediately retreats, completely disappearing inside the shell.

I can't help but laugh. A new tenant occupies my prize shell. A hermit crab beat me to it.

I wait again, holding my palm farther away from my face so as not to frighten the small crab a second time. Wary, the claws come out, the antennae, and then its blue eyes. I surmise that it recently upsized to this spacious shell; its fit resembles a child playing dress-up in her mother's shoes. The crab will not be exchanging this shell for a bigger one any time soon.

Hermit crabs survive by living inside scavenged mollusk shells. Without the shells' protection, the crabs' soft under-bellies make them easy prey. However, as the crabs grow, their shell of choice becomes too tight, making it necessary to a find another, bigger home, which is not always an easy task. In the hermit crab world, there is a housing crisis.

It has been posited that thirty percent of hermit crabs inhabit shells too small for them.[47] The crabs multiply faster than the mollusk shells they inhabit, plus environmental stresses and people collecting shells reduce the supply. I saw a remarkable documentary on BBC Earth about a hermit crab housing chain.[48]

In the documentary, a large, empty shell washes ashore, and a small hermit crab approaches. The small crab real-izes the shell is too spacious for it, but it waits. Soon, other hermit crabs approach and begin measuring each other up. Unbelievably, the crabs start queuing up in an orderly line, like matryoshka dolls, from the smallest to the largest.

Sure enough, as if they all knew it would happen, a larger-than-all-of-them hermit crab approaches. It, too, is in need of a bigger shell. It checks out the new, large empty shell that originally washed ashore, the one that started the whole lineup. The largest crab decides the new, washed-up shell is indeed the perfect size.

An amazing chain reaction begins when the large hermit crab abandons its too-small shell for the larger one. Like fall-ing dominoes, the next-size crab exits its shell and moves into the larger, vacated shell in front of it, then the next crab in line does the same, and the next, and so on. It is spellbind-ing to watch. Somehow, the natural impetus of these crea-tures is to know how and when to find larger living quarters.

I can relate to this need, this imperative, actually, to find a bigger space, a place in the psyche that can accommodate the fullness of our unstoppable unfolding. I believe there is a housing crisis for maturing, untamed women in our youth-oriented culture. Instead of moving into a new space that can accommodate, maybe even celebrate, our maverick spirit, our latent creative potential, the time etched upon our face, and our graying hair of lived experience, we are encouraged to remain in our cramped shell of youth for as long as possible. We dye our hair, Botox our wrinkles, and seek relevance, not in the essence of who we are and what we do, but in doctoring our appearance and minimizing our role. We deny the abundant harvest of our ripening by permitting our relevancy to wither on the vine.

I have no control over aging (or ageism), but I am free to choose where and how I will seek relevance, joy, and meaning in my everyday life. While much may be left behind in our outgrown shells of youth, there await larger shells for the taking, with more space for exploration.

I want to celebrate and bless these housewarmings in myself and others.

Whatever you do, don't live a life too small for you, I would tell my younger self. You will be faced with opportunities to evolve and grow. Risk letting go. Allow yourself to try on new ideas and ways of being in the world. Don't hem yourself in with outmoded beliefs and status-quo thinking. Let the old job go if it holds you back; the old, safe way of doing something if it confines you to a rut; the old tapes if they limit you.

Don't be afraid to be vulnerable as you move from a snug, confining structure into a roomier, not-so-snug place. Like a set of nesting matryoshka dolls, every stage of life offers us an opportunity to grow by shedding limiting views, expectations, and assumptions. Every stage of life offers us an opportunity to expand our psyche and move into a larger space, a space big enough to hold not only life's joys, but also its sorrows and suffering. Ever evolving and growing, the latter stages of life present us with opportunities to multiply our capacity for love, joy, and hope, amid the pain and imperfection of the world.

And, when the time comes, as it surely will, be willing to let go of the limiting ideas about age and your relevance in the world. Queue up in the lineage of wise women before you, seeking larger spaces, to live larger lives.

I peek one last time into the near-perfect, case-worthy tulip shell and carry the hermit crab back into the Gulf. Cool water encircles my thighs as I return it to the rhythm of the sea. I watch it slowly sink. A time will come when this shell, too, will be shed.

Until then . . .

Happy housewarming, my friend!

EARTHING

I'm fairly certain that I am the only one on the beach, this squeaky-bright morning, who believes she is *earthing*. However, the barefoot beachgoers and fishermen around me are earthing, too, either knowingly or unknowingly.

I first stumbled upon the concept of earthing (some call it *grounding*) in an article in the *Journal of Environmental and Public Health*.[49] Basically, earthing enthusiasts believe that people's health fares better when they regularly ground with the earth's electrical charge. I became even more intrigued after I learned that a professional baseball trainer I know uses a grounding mat to enhance healing in some of his players.

Walking barefoot on the earth and swimming in a natural body of water are the easiest and most natural ways to ground. Rubber soles are a no-no. Rubber does not conduct electrical charges, which is why I unlaced my tennis shoes, burrowed my toes into the warm sand, and scooped sand into a mound around my ankle.

If I move my ankle too abruptly, a sharp stab of pain

snatches my breath. The swelling and tendinitis have been slow to heal. I gently massage the area and catch a whiff of the menthol gel I rubbed on earlier. Hard to believe improper shoes caused me so much discomfort. My doctor scolded me for not wearing supportive enough shoes after I admitted to clambering over boulders and down riverbeds while visiting my sisters in Lake Tahoe.

I sigh, lean back into the soft back of my chair, and watch the fishermen, some waist-deep in water and others casting from a rock outcropping. Two boys laugh and splash as they play something akin to king of the mountain on their raft. I relish the idea that my sitting here with my feet resting in the sand benefits my body. I don't mind filling this prescription. (The only thing better would be to discover that eating ice cream would be really good for me, too.)

I wiggle my toes in the damp sand, thinking about invisible electrons and protons. No atom is complete without them. Very simply put, if an atom has an unpaired electron, it becomes a free radical, an unstable and reactive atom that can damage cells and contribute to inflammation and disease. Theoretically, grounding the body allows negative electrons from the earth to enter the body and neutralize positively charged free radicals at the sites of inflammation.[50]

As a young child, I knew nothing of electrons and protons, but I did know the wonder and bliss of walking barefoot on the earth, lying on soft grasses, and wading in cool streams. While I had no name for it, I believe I sensed the subtle transmissions of earth energy to me.

I drew sustenance from nature, and, if I were quiet enough, it seemed to me I could sense a pulsing—something akin to a *heartbeat*. I felt an intimacy with the earth, so much so that when a Jungian analyst once asked me what helped me get through my turbulent childhood, I answered unequivocally, "Mother Nature."

Indigenous cultures around the world have recognized and honored their connection to Mother Earth. French philosopher Frédéric Gros writes about American Indians who held their councils seated on the ground, believing the earth was a sacred source of energy that would afford greater wisdom. In his book, *A Philosophy of Walking*, he writes,

> *The Earth was an inexhaustible well of strength: because it was the original Mother . . . It was the element in which transmission took place. Thus, instead of stretching their hands skyward to implore the mercy of celestial divinities, American Indians preferred to walk barefoot on the Earth.*[51]

Sadly, most every sole of every shoe I own is rubber. I wear tennis shoes on my walks. No earth energy for me. Our modern lifestyle of asphalt, off-ground structures, and rubber-soled shoes inhibits us from making direct contact with the earth. I hope to be more conscious about it going forward, which is why I have taken the time this morning to plant my feet directly on the earth.

I think we could all benefit from our mother's touch.

Steal some moments to "sole" the earth, I would tell my younger self. Find opportunities to peel off your shoes and socks. Bury your toes in sand. Feel the tickle of grass or the warmth of sunbaked clay. Open yourself to the subtle transmissions from this great mother of ours. Let her "soul" you. Perhaps part of what ails our modern world is our disconnect, quite literally, from the earth. Our skyscrap-

ers, asphalt jungles, high-heeled and rubber-soled shoes, deprive us of grounding to the earth's beneficial electromagnetic current.

Don't forget what it felt like as a child to lie with your belly flat to the ground, smelling and hugging the earth when no one was around. The earth's embrace can soothe the soul, touch the heart, and restore the body.

The fishermen and king-of-the-raft boys appear to have no other plans today. I do; I need to make my way upstairs and into my office to write for a while. I brush the gritty sand from my ankle.

Whatever benefit I received from my earthing session is imperceptible, as I expected. I imagine the effect to be cumulative. I don't mind. I welcome an excuse to take a dose of this early-morning medicine: quiet time beside the sea, feet buried in warm sand, sitting beneath an umbrella of blue sky.

Without a doubt, this medicine is also a prescription for happiness.

SEA OATS

The light seems just right this morning.

Mandy, very adept with a camera, investigates the beach with me, looking for a suitable place to snap a profile picture for my website. I have asked for a casual, almost spontaneous pose outdoors—something that reflects me and my love of this place.

Truth be told, I've been feeling slightly uneasy lately about the impending publication of my memoir. Being an introvert, I wince, thinking about the glare of public exposure. I felt very cloistered and protected sitting alone in my office day after day, distilling my feelings and memories onto paper. But now my office walls have fallen away, and my life and thoughts will soon be on public display.

Mandy and I trudge in deep sand toward several dunes, talking about everything and nothing, as we so often do. Our conversations flow as easily as breath, rising and falling. Unsurprisingly, we both see the wild sea oats at the same time. They rise shoulder high, haloed with morning light, their seed-laden heads nodding toward the dunes.

"What do you think?" I ask, brushing my fingertips across the soft, long grasses waving in the breeze.

"Perfect," Mandy says, looking through her lens.

The lacy, delicate appearance of the sea oats belies their hardy nature. Theirs is a fierce beauty. They can weather drought, withstand sand temperatures in excess of 110 degrees, and tolerate salinity. This established clump of oats likely has roots nearly thirty feet long, which help to stabilize the sand around me.

Still, I climb very carefully to the top of the dune so as not to disturb it. Even though these oats are not endangered, Florida laws protect them. Picking the grasses or seeds is illegal because they play such a vital role in protecting and preserving the dunes. And the dunes, in turn, protect the island; they act as sentinels, guarding our shore against storm surges and hurricane-force winds.

Long before I wrote my book, I remember picking up a stalk of sea oats that had fallen on the sand. The oats reminded me of wheat—often a symbol of life and abundance. I had placed the stem of oats next to a candle that I had carried down from the condo for the purpose of offering up a prayer on the beach. At that time, entering the decade of my forties, I was seeking direction and inspiration.

What, I asked the Universe, *does my heart and soul most want to pursue?* I released my question into the gathering night. Later, I collected my belongings, left the oats on the sand, and headed back to our condo.

The next morning something rather extraordinary happened. The timing of it was as uncanny as the event itself.

The precise moment I went for my morning walk, I saw an osprey swoop down, curl its talons, and pluck up the very stem of sea oats I had placed beside my candle the night before. The osprey circled above my head three times gripping the trailing stem and then winged south, toward the channel marker, where it was building a nest with its mate.

I stood there for the longest while. What were the chances that the sea oats I included in my prayer would now line the nest of osprey fledglings? The synchronicity felt like a powerful message and affirmation: with the help of the Universe, my next endeavor would find its way into the world in a beneficial manner. In hindsight, I believe this experience had everything to do with writing my memoir.

So, today, it seems very fitting that Mandy should photograph me in the midst of sea oats. Not only do the sea oats harken back to my prayer, but they also protect and guard the shoreline. Surely if the oats can weather drought, withstand high temperatures, and tolerate salinity, I should be able to weather a little public scrutiny. Writing may be a solitary act, but publication means that a writer's words, thoughts, and feelings go public; they take flight in the universe to land where they may.

"Turn more this way," Mandy says, pointing toward the sea.

I settle close enough to a stalk of oats to breathe in its nutty, grain-like aroma and feel the tickle of it against my cheek. I cannot help but smile. Mandy snaps a picture and then another.

Sitting here on a sand dune, I like to think the look in my eyes is one of gratitude instead of unease. Gratitude for sea oats, osprey, and answered prayer. Gratitude for the people in my life who have helped me, over a lifetime, to send long, stabilizing roots into the shifting sands of time.

Mandy, Jim, my sisters, and friends are the sea oats of my life; their sturdy roots of love and loyalty, entwined with mine, help protect my tender dreams, ready to take flight into the world.

It's important to deepen and strengthen that which protects you, I would tell my younger self. Allow yourself to reach for the sky, but sink hardy roots that can withstand drought, weather storms, and shelter you.

Discover this landscape of fierce beauty within yourself and, when you do, do not trample blindly through it. Pick your way carefully. Sit among the sheaves, remembering who you are and those whose love and devotion helped strengthen you.

Offer up prayers to the Universe and be open to mystery. The soul often speaks in synchronicities; it's a language of happenstance spoken by many things—including sea oats and osprey.

Mandy shows me the pictures. I'm pleased. She captured a slightly weathered woman surrounded by sea oats, a woman who appears to feel at ease and very much at home in her home by the sea.

MANDY'S WEDDING

I snapped a picture of Mandy when she was ten, dressed like a bride. She smiled shyly beneath my old wedding veil, carrying a bouquet of yellowed silk flowers destined for Goodwill. I felt a pang of both love and inevitability. I had the sense I was witnessing a dress rehearsal, albeit decades early.

Twenty-five years later, white satin ribbons, adorning a simple altar, glimmer in the breeze, candle flames flicker, and palm fronds wave and clack in a cloudless sky. Love and hope flutter inside me like butterflies in a garden. Mandy, dressed in a short white dress, carrying a bouquet of fragrant white roses, looks first to me and then to Jim.

Jim's lips quiver. Mandy holds the keys closest to his heart. Years earlier, in the delivery room minutes after her birth, Jim locked eyes with our daughter and lovingly whispered, "You're the most beautiful little girl in the world." He has never stopped believing otherwise.

"You know I don't want a big, fancy ceremony," Mandy had said when we began to discuss her wedding plans. I nodded. Her favorite weddings were small, intimate affairs—just the bride and groom, backdropped by the sea.

And so it is.

Mandy doesn't have sisters, but Jared does. They have come with their children to support Jared. Jared's oldest niece, Brooke, both elegant and graceful, carries a white gladiola down the grassy path and places it on the altar in memory of Jared's mother. The youngest child, Tanner, teeters down the aisle holding a tiny bell that he sometimes remembers to ring, eliciting a smile from all of us. Next, Chatham and Delaney, looking like twin princesses dressed in white, scatter pink rose petals onto the grass.

Then everyone turns to look at Mandy, who is exquisite in her white dress, as the melody of Pachelbel's Canon in D floats outward on harp strings. Jim and I, on either side of her, begin the processional down the grass-path aisle between the palm trees. Each step draws us closer to the sea, toward Jared, our son-in-law-to-be, toward a future in which Mandy and Jared vow to love and cherish each other for the rest of their lives.

We pass the smattering of chairs, kiss Mandy's cheek, and leave her to face Jared. The sun rides low on the western horizon, scattering sea diamonds across the water behind them. With trembling hands, Mandy and Jared read their vows, interjecting a bit of humor. I'm glad for the humor; laughter can cement love into place.

"I promise to love you even when you're hangry," Jared says with a smile. (Mandy gets grumpy when she's hungry.)

"And I promise to always care about the strike zone," Mandy responds. (Jared works in baseball.)

They stand before us, these two, and seal their vows

with a kiss. The years ahead of them lie untouched, like a fresh-washed beach waiting for their footprints. I remember clearly the day Jim and I married, the day we set sail together as a couple. I was twenty and couldn't wait for our life to unfold, full throttle ahead. The years have rushed past in such a blur. I didn't realize, then, the enormity of the love and commitment behind our vows, or how we would be called upon to live them. We are now like two old salts of the sea with miles and miles of adventures behind us, grateful that we weathered the challenges that came our way.

I glance at the empty chair across the aisle from me; the chair and the gladiola on the altar are in memory of Jared's mom. Her life was much too brief. She died in a car accident years ago, leaving behind Jared, who was in college, and his three younger sisters. She has missed many milestones in their lives—college graduations, marriages, and the births of her grandchildren. Still, Jared and his sisters have kept alive an ironclad love for her, and I strongly feel her presence in our midst.

Chatham and Delaney recently asked if they could call me Grandma, since their grandma was in heaven. Of course, I answered yes. I like to believe their heavenly grandmother approves, and I want her to know she can use my arms for hugs whenever she wants. I make her a promise, mother to mother, grandmother to grandmother, to love and nurture our newly blended families.

You do what you can from your world, I tell her, *and I'll do what I can from mine.*

Time is a wily thing, I would tell my younger self. When you're younger, standing at the threshold of new beginnings, years appear to stretch in front of you like a vast sea. But there comes a point, if you are fortunate enough to live a long life, when the sands of the time, sliding toward the bottom of an hourglass, appear to pick up speed, barreling toward an end point you may be reluctant to reach. And, sadly, some hourglasses are smashed, robbing a life of time.

This is why it is imperative to luxuriate in the small eddies of time that present themselves daily. Delight in sunlight sparkling on water, palm fronds clacking in the breeze, the tinkling of a bell, family gatherings, a daughter playing dress-up, a husband's whisperings, even a thousand balls crossing the strike zone. Savor the minutes that shape-change into years; they are points of light, shimmering in the heart, long after youth and life bid farewell.

And, when it comes to the math of love, remember. Allow the years to multiply love. Love should be about addition and multiplication, not division and subtraction. This applies to new family members as well. One family plus one family equals exponential opportunities to multiply love, build new memories, and receive more hugs.

Mandy and Jared wind their way, hands clasped, toward the water's edge for photographs, love filling the space between them. The grandchildren blow and chase the wedding bubbles we handed out after the ceremony. One shiny bubble floats toward Jim and me. I sigh, relieved; I think everything turned out just as Mandy had hoped.

I watch Jared lift Mandy into his arms for a sunset photograph. I squeeze Jim's hand, remembering. May Mandy and Jared arrive on the very shore where Jim and I now stand—on the threshold of our fiftieth anniversary, two old salts still very much in love.

BIG SKY

I love big sky—views encompassing ninety-five percent sky and five percent other—views so expansive they dwarf the ills of this world. Whenever I allow my eyes to traverse the width and breadth of the horizon, some tethered thing in my heart, a holy spark, wakens. It unfurls its wings, lifts majestically into the heavens, and glides on the thermal updrafts inside the clouds, soaring like a frigatebird. My reverence for big sky and shape-shifting clouds culminates every time I participate in one of my favorite pastimes: cloud watching.

Some might consider cloud watching an idle waste of time. I believe differently, which is why I have brought a towel to spread across a chaise lounge. The lounge scrapes across the pavers as I pull it into a patch of shade, compliments of a coconut palm that dips its emerald fronds toward the horizon.

Perfect. Nothing impedes my view of the blue canvas overhead.

Fleecy cumulus clouds slide south over the Gulf. They

look impressionistic, reminiscent of a Monet, painted with short white brushstrokes onto the cerulean sky. Unfurling my beach towel, I lie down. This may be one of my easier New Year's resolutions.

I have resolved to fret less about politics and the state of our world, to remember our adult daughter is perfectly capable of navigating her own life without me white-knuckling a make-believe steering wheel, and to engage in more mindful activities—tai chi, meditation, and, yes, even nephelococcygia (ne-feh-lo-coc-sig-gee-ah), more commonly known as cloud watching. Cloud watching fosters my creativity and well-being.

My birth father, a second-generation cloud watcher and farmer, highly valued the art of studying the sky, not only to play cloud charades, but also to translate cloud language into impending weather, which impacted his crops and livestock, the very cornerstones of his existence. Discerning the height and shapes of the clouds helped my father calculate when to plant, harvest, and round up the herd. He taught me the higher the base of the clouds, the dryer the atmosphere and the fairer the weather.

Cirrus clouds, made of ice crystals, trail like a lock of wispy hair in the upper atmosphere; stratus clouds spread across the sky like a soft blanket; nimbus clouds hang heavy and low, releasing rain or snow; and cumulus clouds, my favorite, resemble feather pillows and down comforters, piled atop one another.

Above me, a cloud shape-shifts into a smiling poodle on top of a giant sea turtle; then, another cloud takes on the shape of a girl with pigtails beside a bear wearing a hat. I savor the deliciousness of lying here beneath the big sky, loitering, contemplating, and letting my imagination create clouds of thought and possibility. I am not a card-carrying member of the Cloud Appreciation Society, a group actually headquartered in the United Kingdom, but I agree with their philosophy: "Clouds are for dreamers and their contemplation benefits the soul."[52]

As a new mother, I tried to pass on the art of cloud watching to Mandy. Many a day we lay shoulder to shoulder on a towel or blanket, pointing out the different shapes of the billowy white silhouettes that paraded across the blue bolt of sky. I remember Mandy's innocence back then, her ability to focus completely on the task at hand. If she spotted a cloud giraffe, that giraffe filled the entirety of her attention. I, on the other hand, had to elbow that very same giraffe into a crowded mind filled with a myriad of different thoughts—some mundane, like writing deadlines, dentist appointments, and class schedules. Other thoughts were more existential, like, what if I'm not living up to my potential, what if something happened to Jim, or, God forbid, what if something happened to Mandy?

So many of the things I fretted and worried about back then never materialized. All of those appearing and disappearing thoughts and emotions traversing across the sky of my mind were like clouds—imagined scenarios and shapes that did little more than rob me of my equanimity.

I can see that much more clearly these days. While I can't halt the parade of thoughts that run through my mind, I'm more adept at recognizing that past and future scenarios hold no more weight or authority than a cloud girl with pigtails or a bear wearing a hat. I need not chase them down a rabbit hole, only observe their passing.

Perhaps a spark in me knows, deep down, that I am ninety-five percent big sky and only five percent other. That's the other side of the cloud-watching coin. It's something Mandy knew as a little girl. If your mind is calm and you see a fluffy white giraffe, you have plenty of room to invite it in.

It's easy to lose our perspective, I would tell my younger self—so easy to forget the expansiveness of our existence. Innumerable clouds have moved across my sky: high, fair-weather clouds; middle, flattened mundane clouds; storm clouds; and clouds piled high, shape-shifting into ten thousand imagined conversations and unfounded worries.

You, dear one, are the spacious sky, not the passing clouds. Never lose sight of this. When you connect with the big sky within, you can weather whatever comes your way. Above the clouds, beyond anxiety and distress, there exists a calm, peaceful, open spaciousness. Soar in those currents. When clouds begin to parade across your mind, become a cloud watcher, an observer; separate yourself from your thoughts. Allow the tethered holy spark within you to lift and join the vast expanse of big sky.

Alas, my serene afternoon of cloud watching draws to a close. I spot a plane contrail overhead and imagine a passenger looking down at the clouds, a perspective no less thrilling.

I remember when Mandy and I vacationed in the big-sky country of New Mexico. We visited the home and studio of famed artist Georgia O'Keeffe. O'Keeffe loved big sky, too. She devoted much of her canvases to painting clouds and sky.

One canvas, her largest, *Sky above Clouds IV*, spanned the entire twenty-four-foot width of her garage. The mural-size painting, depicting dozens of abstract white cumulus clouds from above, was so large it would not fit through any door of San Francisco's Museum of Art,[53] proving one thing:

When you identify with the sky, no small canvas will do.

PRISMS AND RAINBOWS

Fall is coming. I know. And not because my monthly calendar, with its curled edges, has only three pages yet to be clipped to the nine previous pages, marking trips taken, dinners scheduled, and appointments kept.

No. I know fall is imminent because dozens of rainbows sprinkle my dressing area with bands of color. I reach out and twirl a round crystal prism hanging on the inside of my window. A dear and seasoned soul named Ruth gifted it to me more than thirty-five years ago. Since then, it has hung year-round in a window in every house we have owned. I stand back and admire the rainbows still shimmering and dancing across the walls, the floor, and a large white bowl of shells near my washbasin.

Twice a year, near the spring and fall equinoxes, the traversing morning sun slants just so through my east-facing window and strikes the prism. For several weeks of the year, morning rainbows greet me. Whenever I spin the prism, I think of Ruth and the joy she brought into our lives. I remember the trill in her voice and our many conversations about what awaits us on the other side of life. Ruth was not afraid to die. She told me about sitting at the bedside of a dying friend—at the moment of death, her friend looked somewhere beyond Ruth's head, smiled, and whispered, "It's just so beautiful."

Mandy called Ruth *Nanny*, as she was the closest Mandy ever came to having a grandmother. And Nanny called Mandy *my brown-eyed girl*. I remember Mandy's gleeful pirouettes in our kitchen, where the prism first hung, as she tried to capture the dancing bands of color in her small, outstretched hands.

"Do it again, Mommy," she clapped, wide-eyed with wonder, amazed that a piece of glass could transform sunlight into rainbows.

To her delight, I would twirl the prism again and again, cascading a thousand shimmering rainbows across the kitchen cabinets and walls. I took her hands in mine, London bridge–style, and we danced about the kitchen, jeweled colors kissing our faces and arms. Ruth was there sometimes, smiling, eyes shining, admiring the rainbow colors on her own time-worn hands.

I gave little thought, then, to a time, decades down the road, when Ruth would be gone and those very same colors would bathe another pair of time-worn hands—my own. I hold one hand out now, admiring the stripes of a rainbow spread across my skin, pigmented in wavelengths of red, orange, yellow, green, blue, indigo, and, my favorite of the sun's colors, violet.

How is it, really, that sunlight can scatter into such deep and brilliant hues? It was Sir Isaac Newton who suggested that light itself was different colors. Many considered

Newton's concept of the color spectrum radical. It's easy to imagine people's skepticism.

I spend countless hours in daylight, oblivious to the jeweled colors hiding within it. This fact gives me pause. What other radical concepts lie hidden within my days? What other prisms await my marvel?

I didn't learn about quantum physics until after Ruth died. Like me, I think she would have been electrified by the concept of the observer effect, which suggests an observer can impact the outcome of an experiment in the subatomic world.[54] And then Dr. Larry Dossey's book *Recovering the Soul* opened my eyes to the concept of nonlocal mind—the idea that human consciousness is not confined to our brains or our bodies.[55]

For me, these discoveries are like Newton's discovery of the color spectrum. I feel the mystery of them in my bones—something akin to enlightenment. They point to possibility, hope, and awe; they open my heart and forge a connection with what lies beyond.

Look for more than meets the eye, I would tell my younger self. Can you see the wind? Can you measure the depth of love? Can you conjure the impact of a gift decades later? No. So much exists beyond our five senses and awareness. Our earthly bodies are only the tip of the iceberg of who we truly are.

Make room in your life for amazement. Be curious about what can't be seen. Hang prisms of every sort on the windows of your days and witness their revelations. And, by all means, celebrate the ordinary—admire the sun's colors upon your skin; celebrate the arrivals of springs and autumns. Cherish the joy of a little girl twirling in rainbows. Seek to become a seasoned woman, bearing a radical gift in your hand.

Looking at my graying temples in the mirror, I wonder if aging, itself, is a prism, diffusing life into deep and brilliant hues of wisdom and lived experience. I grasp the prism in my fingertips, give it one last twirl, and cause it to scatter a thousand dancing rainbows.

Here's to you, Ruth, wherever you might be.

EPHEMERAL CASTLES
OF SAND

I pause, studying this fortress of sand, first gauging the number of hours spent on its creation and then looking about for its creators.

The four turrets, spiraling to my knees, mark the boundaries of this Lilliputian edifice, complete with a moat and pen-shell drawbridge. Careful hands have etched the sand into a stone facade, complete with a carved archway, connecting the drawbridge to a smooth, sandy courtyard. A lone seagull feather stands erect, its edges fluttering in the breeze, an avian banner heralding make-believe knights and royalty.

Could it be the family of four passing a pretzel bag, beneath an umbrella pied in yellow, green, and blue wedges?

I have an affinity for the human heart that is content to build a sandcastle. The transitory nature of building sandcastles requires the ego to loosen its reins. Legacy, recognition, permanence, and immortality might have a foothold in pyramid building and other forms of creativity, but impermanence, anonymity, creating for the sake of creating, giving an afternoon to an endeavor that will be swept away by the incoming tide—this is the soulfulness of sand sculpture.

Sandcastle builders remind me of crouched Tibetan monks, creating their beautiful, intricate sand mandalas, allowing the world to fall away as they devote their full attention to the gritty sand beneath their fingertips. Their creations testify to the impermanence of existence; in a few hours, or days, their work will disappear, absorbed into oblivion.

This type of creativity touches a place in my soul, which must be why I also love the nature sculptures of Andy Goldsworthy. His temporary masterpieces melt, fall, blow away, and disappear. A photograph is all that remains of his creation. Like holograms, ephemeral creations carry within them the bigger picture that all life is transitory.

Years ago, Mandy and I sat on this very beach, encased in a timeless bubble. My fingers brushed hers as we created a mermaid from grains of sand. We shaped her fishhook tail and mounded breasts beneath a pair of cockle shells. We gathered seaweed for flowing hair and dozens of scallop shells for the scales on her tail.

Mandy chattered on about mermaids. They weren't real, she told me. Could she maybe be one for Halloween? And what if someone stole the shells from the mermaid's tail overnight? In Mandy's mind, the mermaid had taken up residence. I knew it was only a matter of time.

Mandy was unaware of the tide line inching toward us. There could be no stemming of the tide, no preservation of our mermaid or her shell-studded tail, and no bronze casting of my precious mermaid sculptress.

When we stood, finally, to admire our mermaid sand

sculpture, the sun surprised us with its descent into the sea. As the first wave lapped against the mermaid's fanned tail, Mandy frowned and looked up.

Her eyes pierced mine. "Mommy!" she exclaimed.

"I know," I soothed.

And I did know about that moment when we come face-to-face with impermanence, that shattering moment when we recognize that the things we love can be swept away, that moment we discover our powerlessness to stop the tide of time. I felt that ache as a six-year-old when I watched Mama drive away in a cloud of dust; she did not return for two years. Leaving Mandy like that would be unthinkable, but life is fraught with severings, both great and small.

"Our mermaid is going back into the sea," I consoled, "so she can swim with the dolphins."

Mandy leaned into me. I slipped my arm around the warm, tanned shoulders of innocence.

Life, I would tell my younger self, is not so much about creating lasting legacy and posterity, as it is about the devotion and love that go into the creating. All structures rise and fall. Even the great pyramids will eventually disappear into the tide of time. All life is transitory; we are merely passing through. Atoms and cells rising and coming together, like grains of sand, forming and reforming, over and over.

It is tempting to fret about the mortar that gives the illusion of permanence. In reality, love is the mortar. Sandcastles, Tibetan sand mandalas, and other temporary creations strip away the appearance of constancy. They task us with being in the present moment, the only place on earth where eternity dwells. Devotion, from this space, this one "now" moment, is like a prayer, permeating the entire cosmos, leading us to the great hall of love.

The family with the bag of pretzels begins to pack up. Dad folds down the colorful umbrella; Mom shakes sand from the towels and tosses sandy toys into a bucket. The daughter, no older than Mandy when we built our long-ago mermaid, pauses, takes one last look at her castle, and plucks up the white feather. She holds it in her small fist, like a torch, running to rejoin her family.

Forty years and more than fifty thousand tides mark Mandy's passage from childhood to womanhood. Forty years and fifty thousand tides mark my journey from young mother to crone. Forty years and fifty thousand tides, seemingly as brief and ephemeral as a mermaid sculpted of sand, mark my life by the sea.

I wish I could tell my grown-up Mandy, and the young mother tucking the pretzel bag beneath her arm, how quickly this life, with its shifting shorelines, passes. How quickly the tide rushes in.

Listen, I would tell them. . . .

High tide lays smooth the sand,
where a lone gull and I stand.
The sun's exhale colors the horizon.

Silent wings lift upward.
My walk continues northward,
following the curve of the shoreline home.

—TERRY HELWIG

ACKNOWLEDGMENTS

The list of people who have loved, helped, encouraged, guided, and listened to me is much too great to include in its entirety. To you, whose names I carry within my heart, thank you; you have left indelible footprints along the shoreline of my life.

When my sister Nancy Matulich was battling pancreatic cancer, I told her that I planned to dedicate my next book to her. She pulled me close, lovingly squeezed my arm, and whispered, "I had a feeling you might do that." She knew how much I loved her and how much I would miss her. Her footprints and those of my other sisters, Vicki Hess, Patricia Fleming, Brenda Guichu-Polomski, Joni Knauer, and Robin Shaddy, helped shape who I am today.

I am also grateful to my sister friends, Sue Monk Kidd, Trisha Sinnott, and Curly Clark, who give me the Gift of a Day every year; your love and encouragement are invaluable and helped bring this book into fruition. Thank you for your enduring friendship.

My agent, Claire Gerus, who steered this manuscript to

Hannah Bennett, my editor at Viva Editions—I appreciate your enthusiasm and belief in this book. And thanks to Jan Johnson for her early comments and suggestions.

To Leslie Helwig, my friend and sister-in-law; Sue Monk Kidd and Ann Kidd Taylor, family of my heart; and Carolyn Rivers, a dream sister and longtime friend—thank you for carefully poring over my manuscript. Your insightful comments helped, inspired, and encouraged me.

Island residents Paul Reisinger, Candie Simmons, Jackie Romanowicz, Bob McConville, Kent Morse, and Captain Mike Tateo: thank you for brightening my world and allowing me to use your names. Thanks, also, to Mary Ann O'Roark, my friend who stood on her balcony every evening to applaud New York City's front-line workers during the pandemic, and to Patti Boesche, mi amiga y profesora de español. To Paula D'Arcy for her generous praise.

My friends, old and new, who kept checking in with me about the progress of this book from inception to completion—Linda Hardesty-Fish, Carla Riffel, Carol Graf, Alex Beard, Molly Lehman, Betsy Chandler, Diana Crookes, Eirin Connelly, Bobbi Connor, Laurie Steinberg, Dixie Deitchler, Denise George, and my Cozumel family, including my Bocce Babes group—your warm and steady presence means more than you know. Mike and Sondra Hannafan, Pam Nagorske, Joan and Domenic Antonellis, Mary and Bernie Sergesketter, Helen and Chuck Ruth, Linda and Marc Arends, and Sue and Dennis Holewinski—thank you for reaching out, again and again; I treasure your humor and abiding friendship.

To my tribe in CA, NV, TX, IA, NE, AL, MI, IL, KY, OH, DC, FL, NC, MN, CO, NY, and the newly acquired

Porter clan in AZ, MA, and CA, you fill my life with untold love and gladness.

I especially want to thank my husband, Jim, and my daughter, Mandy. You are the sun and moon in my sky. In addition to reading every word many times over, your infinite love, support, and belief in me and my writing are gifts beyond measure.

PONDER THIS
Reader's Guide

A sea of wisdom resides within each of us. Reflection, introspection, and gratitude forge a channel into this sea of knowing. The following questions and suggestions, spawned from themes in this book, offer an opportunity to explore the shifting shorelines of your own life. Just as we listen for the sea inside the spiral of a curved shell, we can listen for the whisper of a wiser self within.

Listening

1. Life is as dynamic and ever-changing as the sea. When viewed through the lens of the imagination, the ordinary can become extraordinary. Take a quiet reprieve from the noise of the outside world to ponder the inner significance of signs, symbols, and synchronicities. Take an imagination walk and suppose that what you see and hear holds special meaning. If something captures your attention, pay attention. What could it symbolize? What concern might it address? (A sea pearl became my talisman for aging, a mangrove propagule my symbol for

writing, and a broken clamshell my reminder to find beauty in the broken.)

2. Put a pen and paper by your bedside and write down one of your dreams upon waking. Dreams are a great resource for tapping into the unconscious. They bypass the ego and speak the language of symbolism and metaphor. Explore and research your dream symbols; when you experience an aha moment, you have tapped into some wiser part of yourself that may offer you an insight about your waking life. (I started a dream group fifteen years ago, which continues to meet, even after I moved away. Jeremy Taylor's books on dream interpretation and how to start a dream group are classics.)

3. Make a collage by pasting different pictures and words/ phrases from magazines, calendars, greeting cards, and photographs onto a piece of poster board. Don't edit anything out. If you're drawn to an image, for whatever reason, include it. Play music while you cut and paste— *feel* your way instead of planning. After you've finished, prop the collage up where you can see it. Study and ponder it. Does something stand out? With my collages, I find that I live into them. Meaning seems to unfold with time, and I am often amazed when a symbol in my collage shows up in real life. (Before I thought of writing *Shifting Shorelines*, I chose a card with a beach scene for my collage, a picture of a seasoned Georgia O'Keeffe, a western sunset, some Winnie the Pooh wisdoms, and a dolphin bracelet. Not until I began writing did I understand what my wiser self knew, long before my waking

self—that I would be incorporating these images in a forthcoming book.)

4. Be creative. The more you engage your imagination, the more it will engage you.

5. Practice mindfulness meditation. Before you begin, dedicate your practice to a person, cause, or solution to a problem. Plan to sit quietly for ten to twenty minutes. Notice the air entering your nostrils on the in breath, and, on each out breath, repeat one or two words of your choice over and over: i.e., *peace, offering love, shining light, radiating health*. When your mind wanders, gently bring it back to your in breath and out breath. Try not to judge your wandering mind; it is like a new puppy not yet trained to take a long walk.

Delight in the Natural World

1. Find a star in the sky, name it, and make up your own constellation story; share it with a child. Instill a sense of wonder about the natural world.

2. Pay attention to the yearly movement of the sun in your corner of the world. What windows, trees, or mountains mark the summer and winter solstices? The winter solstice is a time of drawing in, a time of deepening and quiet. The summer solstice is a time of flinging open the shutters to the soul and wading into the outside world.

3. Dance with the wind, a wave, the sky, or the moon;

dance with abandon and joy. The heart loves to dance with the world.

4. Take a discovery walk. Choose something in your environment that you know little about—a type of tree, an unfamiliar bird, anything in the natural world—and then research it. Learning more about the environment increases our appreciation of the natural world.

Passage of Time

1. If you could write a note about the passage of time to a younger version of yourself, what would you say?

2. Find an object made more beautiful by the patina of time (like my sea pearl). Let this object be a positive talisman for the ripening of wisdom in your own life. Find a special place for your talisman; allow it to remind you that years can polish your soul.

3. Do you have elder role models that you admire? What qualities do you find striking? How can you incorporate some of these qualities into your own life? Have you shared your admiration? If your role model no longer walks in this world, consider writing a belated thank-you and tucking it away somewhere. (I am thinking of my friend's mother who recently passed away at ninety-eight; Leah was a role model for gladness. She volunteered at the hospital, sewed blankets for newborns, and baked cakes and cookies for her extended family. She went about an ordinary day with such cheerfulness that it warmed the hearts of everyone she met, me included.

Her gladness is something I would love to emulate—what a wonderful legacy to leave behind.)

4. Buy yourself a birthday card for the healthy age you hope to reach. Put the card where you will see it often and visualize celebrating this birthday with your loved ones. See yourself blowing out numeral candles of your hoped-for age. (I am an optimist; I see myself blowing out three candles: one, zero, two.)

Friendship

1. Start a friendship group. Friendships provide a safe harbor for emergence. The collective support and wisdom of a group of long-standing friends can help one more easily navigate the shifting shorelines of life. In the chapter *The Gift of Days*, I disclose how three of my out-of-state girlfriends and I gather once a year to give each other the gift of one day each. We have been meeting for sixteen years. (During COVID-19 we improvised and Zoomed four hours a day, for four days.) This format has worked beautifully in our lives, but if time does not permit for such a generous gift, the format can be modified. A monthly or quarterly gathering for a half day, an hour, or half hour could work, too. The idea is to give each member (three to four is an ideal number) the floor, for the allotted time, to use in whatever way they wish—to talk, to share, to ask questions, to brainstorm. All the attention and focus is on the one who has the floor; the only goal of others in the circle is to listen and, if asked, to offer brief thoughts, insights, and feedback. To be listened to so intently is a gift beyond measure.

2. Start or join a group around a common interest, i.e., tennis, pickleball, golf, mah-jongg, dreams, books—the list goes on and on. I value my Bocce Babes group; we have been meeting and playing bocce for years. However, if it were not for the foresight and invitation from our founder, Joan, I doubt the group would exist. Gathering, sharing, bonding, and caring—these are the benefits of joining a group. The feeling of belonging waters the soul.

4. Think about writing important dates in the lives of your friends on a friendship calendar. Is someone facing surgery, celebrating a milestone, supposed to go on an important trip? I have been quite touched when a friend remembers, checks in, and says, *I'll be thinking of you today.*

Be the Change

1. "Be the change you want to see happen." [56] There is no universal *they* in charge of making the world a better place. *We* are the *they*. What issues concern you most? Is there something you can do, however infinitesimal, that would point toward the change you wish to see? Rescuing a bird, picking up litter, speaking up, saving a conch; what small act of kindness is yours to give? Ask yourself, *What one thing could I do this week that might change me?*

2. Send positive energy into the world. What if thoughts have a quantum impact? It costs nothing to send positive energy into the world; it can be released, right now, this very minute, from wherever we sit. Consider turning a

recurring negative thought into an affirmation. For example: *The world is going crazy* is a negative thought. A positive counterpoint might be: *I picture the world transitioning into a kinder place.* (Notice if you feel a difference in your body when you say an affirmation versus a negative thought.)

3. Think of people in your life that *walk their talk*. When a situation arises that opens the door to take action, to be gentler, or to exercise patience, ask, *What would so-and-so do?* (My sister Nancy, who passed away, had a fierce spirit and a soft heart. Sometimes, to encourage myself to act more boldly, I ask, *What would Nancy do?*)

Compassion

1. Interestingly, it is difficult to feel compassion toward others if we do not feel compassion toward ourselves. The cool stare we use to judge another is often the same one that we cast upon ourselves. Stand in front of a mirror and look deeply into your eyes. Allow the self behind your eyes to look upon your face—not with judgment, but with unconditional love. With soft eyes, name three qualities you most admire about the human being standing before you.

2. With that same gaze, picture the face of someone in your life, someone in need of unconditional love instead of judgment. Name three qualities you most admire about that human being.

3. If you find it hard to feel compassionate toward someone, picture this person as a young, lost child—maybe even

your child. In your imagination, put your arm around this child's shoulder and point upward toward a light, a light that bathes the two of you in unconditional love.

Grief

1. The chapter *Otter Mound* is about letting go of grief and sadness; there is mention of a strangler fig that eventually kills its host tree. Is there something in your life that needs to be laid to rest so that it no longer strangles your joy? If so, write a letter saying goodbye to the tentacles of grief that strangle joy, then tear up the letter or burn it.

2. Bury something that symbolizes a debilitating grief or sadness. Say, in parting, the words you most need to hear to move forward. Life is for living.

3. Moving forward is not forgetting loved ones. Moving forward is honoring loved ones. Only through you can loved ones live on. Your joy can be their joy.

Prayer

1. I have what I call a heavenly choir. My heavenly choir is quite large; it consists of departed loved ones, ancestors I don't know, sages, saints, Great Spirit, and the many lamps of the One Light. When I offer up a prayer, it is to this heavenly choir that I call upon. One of my favorite kinds of prayer is to dedicate a specific activity (like playing the harp) as a prayer for a particular person. Playing an instrument, cooking, painting, exercising—all take on more gravitas and meaning if offered up as a prayer.

2. Buy a prayer candle. Light it and leave it burning for a time for the person you are praying for. (Sometimes I write down the name of the person or pull out a photograph and place it beside the burning candle.)

3. Our family also writes notes and prayers on an erasable menu board that we keep out on the kitchen counter. (The person whose name is currently written on the board is undergoing brain surgery this very minute. She does not know that we are praying for her, but we know it.)

4. Take a prayer walk. Imagine that every footfall is a prayer, offered up for the benefit of the earth and all beings.

Gratitude

1. Gratitude opens the heart. Select a gratitude journal and fill it with blessings large and small. Thousands of gifts are bequeathed to us on a daily basis. Things like: lying beside my daughter during an eclipse; watching, amused, as my husband snaps his two hundredth sunset photograph; holding my half of a friendship shell; or watching the shadow of a manatee gliding silently beneath the water. A gratitude journal magnifies the everyday miracles of life. (A friend of mine keeps a gratitude journal open on her kitchen counter, where she and her husband can write in it every day.)

2. Try to express gratitude even during difficult times. Sometimes a seemingly wrong turn becomes a right turn. Think of a disappointment that turned out for the best.

3. Take a gratitude walk. Quietly give thanks to everything you encounter. Give thanks for the sky, clouds, people, animals, and the earth beneath your feet. Notice if there is a difference in your mood before and after the walk.

4. *Life is good*, a friend and I often tell each other, even when experiencing a tough time. What we really mean is that we are grateful for the precious gift of life, even with its inherent challenges, suffering, and disappointments. Select a gratitude saying of your own. Make it yours. Tuck it inside your gratitude journal.

As you ponder the tides and the shifting shoreline of your own life, may the ripening of wisdom continue.

ENDNOTES

1   My sister Nancy and I repeated this line to one another before she died. It is loosely based on Coleman Barks's translation of Rumi. Audio: https://poetshouse.org/audio/2011-coleman-barks-on-rumis-out-beyond-ideas-of-wrongdoing-and-rightdoing/, accessed October 9, 2020.

2   Maulana Jalalu-d-Din Muhammad Rumi, *Masnavi I Ma'navi: The Spiritual Couplets of* Maulana Jalalu-d-Din Muhammad Rumi, Second Edition, trans. E. H. Whinfield (London: Kegan Paul, Trench, Trubner & Co. Ltd, 1898), 138, https://www.google.com/books/edition/Masnavi_i_Ma_navi/0dLXWB5DeIC?hl=en&gbpv=1&dq=Masnavi_i_Ma_navi.html&printsec=frontcover#spf=1607032168748.

3   Rainer Maria Rilke, "To Clara Rilke, March 27, 1903" in *Letters of Rainer Maria Rilke 1892-1910*, trans. Jane Bannard Greene and Herter Norton (New York: W. W. Norton & Company, Inc., 1945), letter 42, 94, https://archive.org/details/lettersofrainerm030932mbp/page/n97/mode/2up

4   Dr. Henri Weimerskirch and colleagues, "Frigate birds track atmospheric conditions over months-long transoceanic flights," *Science* (July 1, 2016): as quoted in *Christian Science Monitor*, Jason Thomson, "Extreme aviators: How do frigatebirds stay aloft for months at a time?" July 1, 2016, https://www.csmonitor.com/Science/2016/0701/Extreme-aviators-How-do-frigatebirds-stay-aloft-for-months-at-a-time.

5   Daniel Austin, *Florida Ethnobotany* (Boca Raton: CRC, 2004), 156, https://books.google.com/books?id=7qgPCEiI4WMC&p

g=PP4&dq=%E2%80%9CQuinine+of+the+poor%E2%80%.

6   Belinda Waymouth, "Ocean Plastic Estimated at 5.25 Trillion Pieces," *Our World*, December 11, 2014, accessed May 2, 2020, https://ourworld.unu.edu/en/ocean-plastic-estimated-at-5-25-trillion-pieces-but-wheres-the-rest.

7   "Information About Sea Turtles: Threats from Marine Debris," *Sea Turtle Conservancy*, accessed May 2, 2020, https://conserve-turtles.org/information-sea-turtles-threats-marine-debris/.

8   *Agence France-Presse,* "Whale dies from eating more than 80 plastic bags," *The Guardian,* June 2, 2018, accessed May 2, 2020, https://www.theguardian.com/environment/2018/jun/03/whale-dies-from-eating-more-than-80-plastic-bags.

9   Frye, Mary. "Do Not Stand at My Grave and Weep." In public domain: http://www.thehypertexts.com/mary%20eliza-beth%20frye%20poet%20poetry%20picture%20bio.htm

10 Laura Layden, "Hurricane Irma's blow to Collier County's beaches: $35 million," *Naples Daily News*, September 25, 2017, https://www.naplesnews.com/story/weather/hurricanes/2017/09/25/hurricane-irmas-blow-collier-countys-beaches-35-million/700452001/.

11 Lindbergh, Anne Morrow. *Gift from the Sea* (New York: Pantheon Books, 1955, 1975), 74-75.

12 Bobby Monroe, "Burmese python captured in Marco Island Community," interview on NBC2 news, accessed on YouTube May 1, 2020, YouTube: https://youtu.be/f7yojBXgmz0.

13 FAQ, "How have invasive pythons impacted Florida ecosystems?" United States Geological Survey (USGS), accessed May 1, 2020, https://www.usgs.gov/faqs/how-have-invasive-pythons-impacted-florida-ecosystems?qt-news_science_products=0#qt-news_science_products.

14 "Python Elimination Program," South Florida Water Management District, accessed May 1, 2020, https://www.sfwmd.gov/our-work/python-program.

15 FAQ, USGS. https://www.usgs.gov/faqs/how-many-bur-mese-pythons-inhabit-southern-florida?qt-news_science_products=0#qt-news_science_products.

16 Rosie Burr, "The Sea Glass and Mermaid's Tears," June 21, 2014, *All at Sea*, accessed May 14, 2020, https://www.allatsea.net/the-sea-glass-and-mermaids-tears/.

17 Nestor Montoya, "Local gun shops see spikes in AR-15 sales after school shooting," NBC2, accessed December 5, 2020, https://youtu.be/ADJ-SQDiB6U

18 David Yaffe-Bellany, "Bulletproof Backpacks in Demand for Back-to-School Shopping," *The New York Times*, August 6, 2019, https://www.nytimes.com/2019/08/06/business/bulletproof-backpack.html?auth=login-email&login=email.

19 "Bald Eagle Biology," U.S. Fish & Wildlife Service, last updated May 5, 2020, https://www.fws.gov/midwest/eagle/Nhistory/biologue.html.

20 "Red-tide Timeline," *Herald-Tribune*, July 16, 2006, accessed May 7, 2020, https://www.heraldtribune.com/news/20060716/red-tide-timeline.

21 Harriet Beecher Stowe, *Uncle Tom's Cabin or, Life Among the Lowly*, Volume Two (Bedford: Applewood Books, 1852), 243, https://books.google.com/books/about/Uncle_Tom_s_Cabin.html.

22 Philip Perry, "Searching for meaning in your life? This Japanese concept can help you find it," February 6, 2018, bigthink.com, https://bigthink.com/philip-perry/searching-for-meaning-in-your-life-this-japanese-concept-can-help-you-find-it.

23 Dalai Lama, Desmond Tutu, with Douglas Carlton Abrams, *The Book of Joy: Lasting Happiness in a Changing World* (New York: Avery, 2016), 14.

24 "Reward Increases to More than $50,000, Cases of Florida Dolphins Shot and Stabbed," NOAA Fisheries, March 2, 2020, https://www.fisheries.noaa.gov/feature-story/reward-increases-more-50000-cases-florida-dolphins-shot-and-stabbed.

25 "Recreational Sea Shell Collecting," Florida Fish and Wildlife Commission, accessed May 27, 2020, https://myfwc.com/search/#?cludoquery=Harvesting%20live%20shells&cludopage=1&cludorefurl=https%3A%2F%2Fmyfwc.com%2F&cludorefpt=Florida%20Fish%20and%20Wildlife%20Conservation%20Commission%20%7C%20FWC.

26 "Beaufort Wind Scale," National Weather Service, National Oceanic and Atmospheric Administration, accessed May 22, 2020, https://www.weather.gov/mfl/beaufort.

27 "Beaufort Wind Scale."

28 Antoine de Saint-Exupéry, *The Little Prince* (New York: Harcourt Brace Jovanovich, Inc., 1943, 1961), 46.

29 Anna Sofaer, "The Primary Architecture of the Chacoan Culture," *A Cosmological Expression,* accessed June 1, 2020, https://solsticeproject.org/images/pdfs/24-Lekson_Chapter_9%2520%25282007%2529.pdf.

30 "Veterans Memorial," Anthem Community Council, accessed June 1, 2020, https://www.onlineatanthem.com/visitors/veterans_memorial/index.php.

31 "Ecclesiastes 3:1-4," King James Bible online, https://m.kingjamesbibleonline.org/Ecclesiastes-Chapter-3/.

32 "The Return: Paradise Found: 6,000 Years of People on Marco Island," Collier County Museums, accessed June 1, 2020, https://colliermuseums.com/exhibits/key-marco-cat-and-other-artifacts.

33 "Florida Panther," National Wildlife Federation, accessed June 1, 2020, https://www.nwf.org/Educational-Resources/Wildlife-Guide/Mammals/Florida-Panther.

34 "Sea Turtles," National Ocean Service, National Oceanic and Atmospheric Administration, U.S. Department of Commerce, accessed June 2, 2020, https://oceanservice.noaa.gov/news/june15/sea-turtles.html.

35 "Sea Turtles."

36 "Anne Hutchinson," edited by Debra Michals, National Women's History Museum, 2015, https://www.womenshistory.org/education-resources/biographies/anne-hutchinson.

37 Arthur Gordon, "The Day at the Beach," in *Everyday Greatness: Inspiration for a Meaningful Life*, commentary by Stephen R. Covey, compiled by David K. Hatch (Nashville: Rutledge Hill Press, 2006), 418.

38 "Saharan Dust Blows Across the Atlantic," Satellite and Information Service, National Oceanic and Atmospheric Administration, June 29, 2018, https://www.nesdis.noaa.gov/content/saharan-dust-blows-across-atlantic.

39 Bernd Wursig, William F. Perrin, J. G. M. Thewissen, eds., *Encyclopedia of Marine Mammals*, second edition (Boston: Academic Press, 2009), 448.

40 "James 1:19," New International Version, Bible Gateway, accessed February 2, 2021, https://www.biblegateway.com/passage/?search=James%201%3A19-20&version=NIV

41 "A Pagan History of the Camino," *Iberian Adventures*, September 17, 2014, https://www.iberianadventures.com/a-pagan-history-of-the-camino/.

42 Mevlana Jalaluddin Rumi, "One, One, One," translated by Andrew Harvey, in *The Rumi Collection*: An Anthology of Translations of Mevlana Jalaluddin Rumi, ed. Kabir Helminski (Boston: Shambhala, 2000), 112, accessed February 2, 2021, https://www.google.com/books/edition/The_Rumi_Collection/l0A-RskdsGu8C?hl=en&gbpv=1&dq=The+lamps+are+different+%22The+lamps+are+different%22+inauthor:Rumi&pg=PA112&printsec=frontcover

43 "Row, Row, Row Your Boat," Lyte, 1881, *The Franklin Square Song Collection*, accessed May 5, 2020, https://en.m.wikipedia.org/wiki/Eliphalet_Oram_Lyte.

44 "Shark attack confirmed on Marco Island; rare in SWFL," *Wink News*, April 27, 2015, https://www.winknews.com/2015/04/27/shark-attack-confirmed-on-marco-island-rare-in-swfl/.

45 Patricia Wuest, "The Dacor Scuba Reg Behind Darth Vader's Breathing," *Scuba Diving,* October 29, 2015, accessed October 7, 2020, https://www.scubadiving.com/dacor-scuba-reg-behind-darth-vaders-breathing.

46 Robert Twilley & Andre Rovai, "Why protecting 'blue carbon' storage is crucial to fighting climate change," *GreenBiz*, accessed July 10, 2020, https://www.greenbiz.com/article/why-protecting-blue-carbon-storage-crucial-fighting-climate-change.

47 Elizabeth Demaray, "Attempting to Meet the New Needs of Natural Life-Forms," *Cabinet*, Issue 13, Spring 2004, accessed July 16, 2020, http://www.cabinetmagazine.org/issues/13/demaray.php.

48 BBC Earth, Life Story, "Hermit Crab House Swap," accessed July 15, 2020, http://www.bbc.com/earth/story/20141103-hermit-crab.

49 Chevalier, Gaétan et al. "Earthing: health implications of reconnecting the human body to the Earth's surface electrons." *Journal of Environmental and Public Health*, vol. 2012 (2012): 291541. doi:10.1155/2012/291541.

50 Chevalier, "Earthing."

51 Frédéric Gros, *A Philosophy of Walking* (London: Verso, 2014), 104.

52 "Cloud Appreciation Society Manifesto," Cloud Appreciation Society, accessed May 9, 2020, https://cloudappreciationsociety.org/manifesto/.

53 "Sky above Clouds IV," Georgia O'Keeffe, the Art Institute of Chicago, accessed May 12, 2020, https://www.artic.edu/artworks/100858/sky-above-clouds-iv.

54 Weizmann Institute of Science, "Quantum Theory Demonstrated: Observation Affects Reality," *Science Daily*, February 27, 1998, accessed January 13, 2021, https://www.sciencedaily.com/releases/1998/02/980227055013.htm.

55 Larry Dossey, MD, biography, accessed January 13, 2021, http://larrydosseymd.com/recovering-the-soul-a-scientific-and-spiritual-search/

56 Lorrance, Arleen, "The Love Project," in *Developing Priorities and a Style: Selected Readings in Education for Teachers and Parents*, edited by Richard Dean Kellough (New York: MSS Information Corporation, 1974), 85.

ABOUT THE AUTHOR

Terry Helwig authored the award-winning *Moonlight on Linoleum*, a coming-of-age memoir about her turbulent, childhood struggle to keep hope alive. A naturalist at heart, with a master's degree in counseling psychology, Helwig credits nature and synchronicity as being two of her most profound teachers. One of her favorite pastimes includes combing the beach of a Florida barrier island, where she resides with her husband, Jim.

Visit: www.terryhelwig.com

Author photo by Jeff Carsten.